Third Workshop on Metaphor in NLP 2015

Held at NAACL HLT 2015

Denver, Colorado, USA
5 June 2015

ISBN: 978-1-5108-0434-0

Printed from e-media with permission by:

Curran Associates, Inc.
57 Morehouse Lane
Red Hook, NY 12571

Some format issues inherent in the e-media version may also appear in this print version.

Printed by Curran Associates, Inc. (2015)

For permission requests, please contact the Association for Computational Linguistics at the address below.

Association for Computational Linguistics
209 N. Eighth Street
Stroudsburg, Pennsylvania 18360

Phone: 1-570-476-8006
Fax: 1-570-476-0860

acl@aclweb.org

Additional copies of this publication are available from:

Curran Associates, Inc.
57 Morehouse Lane
Red Hook, NY 12571 USA
Phone: 845-758-0400
Fax: 845-758-2634
Email: curran@proceedings.com
Web: www.proceedings.com

Introduction

Characteristic to all areas of human activity (from poetic to ordinary to scientific) and, thus, to all types of discourse, metaphor becomes an important problem for natural language processing. Its ubiquity in language has been established in a number of corpus studies and the role it plays in human reasoning has been confirmed in psychological experiments. This makes metaphor an important research area for computational and cognitive linguistics, and its automatic identification and interpretation indispensable for any semantics-oriented NLP application.

This year's workshop is the third Metaphor in NLP workshop, following the first workshop held at NAACL 2013 and the second workshop held at ACL 2014. In 2013, accepted papers dealt with metaphor annotation, features for metaphor identification, and with generalization of the techniques across languages. These themes were also represented in the 2014 workshop, along with interpretation, applications, and relationships with related phenomena. In 2015, prominent themes include creation and utilization of semantic resources for metaphor identification and interpretation; features for metaphor identification that capture properties of concepts such as concreteness, imageability, affect, and sensorial modalities; relationships between social dynamic and individual history and metaphor use; and metaphor generation. We received 13 submissions and accepted 10, based on detailed and careful reviews by members of the Program Committee.

Creation and utilization of semantic resources to support metaphor identification is a recurrent theme in the 2015 workshop. An invited talk by Prof. Martha Palmer and Dr. Susan Brown about metaphor in VerbNet was followed by a number of contributions describing the creation of resources in support of metaphor identification and analysis. Li, Bai ,Yin, and Xu describe the construction of a resource where salient properties of concepts expressed by thousands of Chinese verbs and nouns are collected. Dodge, Hong, and Stickles describe MetaNet, a system combining a repository of metaphors and frames, and a metaphor detection component that utilizes the repository. Gordon, Jobbs, May, and Morbini describe an enhancement to their knowledge-based metaphor identification system that infers lexical axioms – rules which encode information about what words or phrases trigger particular source and target concepts.

Gordon, Hobbs, May, Mohler, Morbini, Rink, Tomlinson, and Wertheim describe their ontology of commonly used source domains and release a corpus of manually validated annotations of linguistic metaphors about governance, economy, and gun control with source and target domains, as well as specific roles (slots) that support the interpretation of the metaphor. For example, according to the ontology, a metaphor drawing on the source domain of JOURNEY can be annotated with elements such as source, target, agent, goal, facilitator, barrier, change, and type of change (increase or decrease). The goal of the dataset is to support the analysis of ways in which a person or a group conceives of a target concept.

A similar goal is a starting point of the contribution by Shaikh, Strzalkowski, Taylor, Lien, Liu, Broadwell, Feldman, Yarrom, Cho, and Peshkova. The authors exemplify the use of their system for detection of linguistic metaphors and their source-target interpretation to analyze the metaphorical content of a specific debate (gun control in the U.S.). Having identified documents on both sides of the debate and the main points of disagreement, they show that the two sides use different metaphors to argue their cause. In conjunction with measures of influence and centrality, the authors show that the kinds of metaphors used and their variety can help to determine the dominant side in the debate. Moving from social to personal, Jang, Wen, and Rose shed light on the relationship between the personal history of a participant in an online discussion forum and their use of metaphor.

Beigman Klebanov, Leong, and Flor describe supervised learning experiments aimed at identifying all content-word linguistic metaphors in a corpus of argumentative essays and in the VU Amsterdam corpus, addressing specifically the impact of features related to concreteness. Concreteness, imageability and affective meanings are also modeled in the contribution by Gargett and Barnden. Tekiroglu, Ozbal, and Strapparava evaluate sensorial features for predicting metaphoricity of adjective-noun constructions, deriving their features from Senticon – a lexicon of words annotated for their association with different sensorial modalities, such as taste or smell.

The contribution by T. Veale presents an automated system for generating metaphors; the evaluation shows that people found about half the metaphors to be highly novel, and about 15% – worthy of sharing with other people.

We wish to thank everyone who showed interest and submitted a paper, all of the authors for their contributions, the members of the Program Committee for their thoughtful reviews, the invited speaker and panelists for sharing their perspectives on the topic, and all the attendees of the workshop. All of these factors contribute to a truly enriching event!

Workshop co-chairs:
Ekaterina Shutova, University of Cambridge, UK
Beata Beigman Klebanov, Educational Testing Service, USA
Patricia Lichtenstein, University of California, Merced, USA

Organizers:

Ekaterina Shutova, University of Cambridge, UK
Beata Beigman Klebanov, Educational Testing Service, USA
Patricia Lichtenstein, University of California, Merced, USA

Program Committee:

John Barnden, University of Birmingham, UK
Yulia Badryzlova, Higher School of Economics, Moscow, Russia
Danushka Bollegala, University of Liverpool, UK
Paul Cook, University of New Brunswisk, Canada
Gerard de Melo, Tsinghua University, China
Ellen Dodge, ICSI, UC Berkeley, USA
Jonathan Dunn, Illinois Institute of Technology, USA
Anna Feldman, Montclair State University, USA
Michael Flor, Educational Testing Service, USA
Mark Granroth-Wilding, University of Cambridge, UK
Yanfen Hao, Hour Group Inc., Calgary, Alberta, Canada
Felix Hill, University of Cambridge, UK
Jerry Hobbs, USC ISI, USA
Eduard Hovy, Carnegie Mellon University, USA
Hyeju Jang, Carnegie Mellon University, USA
Valia Kordoni, Humboldt University Berlin, Germany
Alex Lascarides, University of Edinburgh, UK
Mark Lee, University of Birmingham, UK
Annie Louis, University of Edinburgh, UK
Saif Mohammad, National Research Council Canada, Canada
Behrang Mohit, Carnegie Mellon University, Qatar
Michael Mohler, Language Computer Corporation, USA
Preslav Nakov, Qatar Computing Research Institute, Qatar
Srini Narayanan, Google, Switzerland
Ani Nenkova, University of Pennsylvania, USA
Yair Neuman, Ben Gurion University, Israel
Malvina Nissim, University of Groningen, The Netherlands
Thierry Poibeau, Ecole Normale Superieure and CNRS, France
Bryan Rink, LCC, USA
Eyal Sagi, Northwestern University, USA
Sabine Schulte im Walde, University of Stuttgart, Germany
Samira Shaikh, SUNY Albany, USA
Caroline Sporleder, University of Trier, Germany
Mark Steedman, University of Edinburgh, UK
Gerard Steen, University of Amsterdam, The Netherlands

Carlo Strapparava, Fondazione Bruno Kessler, Italy
Tomek Strzalkowski, SUNY Albany, USA
Marc Tomlinson, LCC, USA
Yulia Tsvetkov, Carnegie Mellon University, USA
Peter Turney, National Research Council Canada, Canada
Tony Veale, University College Dublin, Ireland
Aline Villavicencio, Federal University of Rio Grande do Sul, Brazil
Andreas Vlachos, University College London, UK

Invited Speakers:

Martha Palmer, University of Colorado, Boulder, USA
Susan Windisch Brown, University of Colorado, Boulder, USA
James Martin, University of Colorado, Boulder, USA

Table of Contents

Conference Program

Friday, June 5, 2015

9:00–9:05

+ ***Opening remarks***

9:05–10:05

+ ***Invited talk: Martha Palmer, Susan Brown and Jim Martin "Metaphor in lexical resources"***

10:05–10:30

Effects of Situational Factors on Metaphor Detection in an Online Discussion Forum
Hyeju Jang, Miaomiao Wen and Carolyn Rose

10:30–11:00

+ ***Coffee break***

11:00–11:25

Supervised Word-Level Metaphor Detection: Experiments with Concreteness and Reweighting of Examples
Beata Beigman Klebanov, Chee Wee Leong and Michael Flor

Friday, June 5, 2015 (continued)

11:25–11:50

Modeling the interaction between sensory and affective meanings for detecting metaphor
Andrew Gargett and John Barnden

11:50–12:15

Exploring Sensorial Features for Metaphor Identification
Serra Sinem Tekiroglu, Gözde Özbal and Carlo Strapparava

12:15–12:40

MetaNet: Deep semantic automatic metaphor analysis
Ellen Dodge, Jisup Hong and Elise Stickles

12:40–14:15

\+ ***Lunch***

14:15–14:40

High-Precision Abductive Mapping of Multilingual Metaphors
Jonathan Gordon, Jerry Hobbs, Jonathan May and Fabrizio Morbini

Friday, June 5, 2015 (continued)

14:40–15:05

A Corpus of Rich Metaphor Annotation
Jonathan Gordon, Jerry Hobbs, Jonathan May, Michael Mohler, Fabrizio Morbini, Bryan Rink, Marc Tomlinson and Suzanne Wertheim

15:05–15:30

Understanding Cultural Conflicts using Metaphors and Sociolinguistic Measures of Influence
Samira Shaikh, Tomek Strzalkowski, Sarah Taylor, John Lien, Ting Liu, George Aaron Broadwell, Laurie Feldman, Boris Yamrom, Kit Cho and Yuliya Peshkova

15:30–16:00

\+ ***Coffee break***

16:00–16:25

Chinese CogBank: Where to See the Cognitive Features of Chinese Words
Bin Li, Xiaopeng Bai, Siqi Yin and Jie Xu

16:25–16:50

Fighting Words and Antagonistic Worlds
Tony Veale

Effects of Situational Factors on Metaphor Detection in an Online Discussion Forum

Hyeju Jang, Miaomiao Wen, and Carolyn Penstein Rosé
Language Technologies Institute
Carnegie Mellon University
Pittsburgh, PA 15213, USA
{hyejuj, mwen, cprose}@cs.cmu.edu

Abstract

Accurate metaphor detection remains an open challenge. In this paper, we explore a new type of clue for disambiguating terms that may be used metaphorically or literally in an online medical support community. In particular, we investigate the influence of situational factors on propensity to employ the metaphorical sense of words when they can be used to illustrate the emotion behind the experience of the event. Specifically we consider the experience of stressful illness-related events in a poster's recent history as situational factors. We evaluate the positive impact of automatically extracted cancer events on a metaphor detection task using data from an online cancer forum. We also provide a discussion of specific associations between events and metaphors, such as *journey* with diagnosis or *warrior* with chemotherapy.

1 Introduction

In this paper we present a novel approach to metaphor detection that leverages situational factors in the life of a speaker that alter the propensity to employ the metaphorical sense of specific terms. In recent years, the field of language technologies has made advances in the area of metaphor detection by leveraging some linguistic regularities such as lexical selection, lexical co-occurrence, and abstractness versus concreteness. On the other hand, we know that metaphor is creative at its core, and these linguistic regularities, though essential, are bounded in their ability to enable accurate metaphor detection in a broad sense. In contrast to previous approaches focusing on these linguistically inspired features, we begin to explore situational factors coming from a pragmatic perspective, related to the reasons why people choose to use metaphors. The situational factors may provide a complementary set of indicators to partner with tried and true linguistically inspired features in order to increase performance. Specifically, we explore expressions of metaphors used in a cancer support community in connection with discussion around stressful cancer events. In particular, we provide evidence that propensity to employ metaphorical language increases around the time of stressful cancer events.

Describing an experience metaphorically is an effective conversational strategy for achieving social goals that are relevant within an online medical support community. For example, a metaphor may be useful for drawing the listener closer by revealing not just what has been experienced, but how the speaker is personally engaged with the event, such as *journey* and *battle* (Jang et al., 2014). For example, the *journey* metaphor conveys the experience of cancer treatment as a process of progressing along a path in which the cancer patient is a traveler, whereas the *battle* metaphor conveys a more active attitude towards cancer treatment by comparing cancer treatment to conflict and war where the speaker is positioned as a warrior. In this way, metaphors may be used to build solidarity or a sense of camaraderie as they increase insight into the speaker's personal experience and thus facilitate empathetic understanding between the participants (Ritchie, 2013).

Beyond the social implications of using a metaphor, there are implications at the cognitive level as well. In particular, metaphor is a type of linguistic tool used to express an abstraction. As

Proceedings of the Third Workshop on Metaphor in NLP, pages 1–10,
Denver, Colorado, June 5, 2015.

such, usage of metaphor requires somewhat more cognitive effort than the equivalent literal description. Usage of a metaphor may thus reflect the effort the speaker has invested in making sense out of the associated experience.

Both cognitive and social factors may contribute towards an elevated level of usage of specific metaphors that are associated with the experience of a stressful cancer event in the recent past of a speaker. Specifically, speakers experience a need for more social support during and soon after a stressful event, and thus may engage in behaviors that are useful for building closeness and drawing others in. Additionally, as part of the coping process, experiencers of stressful cancer events are faced with the need to adjust to a new reality after the experience, and this adjustment process may be reflected in linguistic mechanisms that are associated with abstraction and reasoning. Leveraging this insight, we hypothesize that for ambiguous terms (those that can be used either in a literal or metaphorical sense), the concentration of metaphorical use will be elevated within a short window of time following the experience of the associated cancer events. We thus hypothesize that a context variable associated with these events will be a useful clue for increasing accuracy at disambiguating the interpretation of these terms.

In this paper, we present a corpus analysis of data extracted from an online medical support community, where technology has been deployed to extract mentions of specific cancer events (e.g. diagnosis, chemotherapy, etc.). First, we investigate how popular metaphors we find to be unambiguous in our data from the discussion forum are used in connection with major cancer events. This validates the proposed association between cancer events and metaphor usage. Second, we evaluate the extent to which event information can be helpful for a computational metaphor disambiguation task over more ambiguous candidate metaphor words. In this work, we quantitatively verify the effectiveness of considering situational features in metaphor detection.

The major contribution of this work from a computational perspective is to introduce novel types of features for automatic metaphor detection. Metaphor is not a purely linguistic phenomenon only, but it is language in use. It can depend on a variety of factors including the mood, audience, identity of speaker, and the situational context of the speaker. Thus, we believe that combining insights both from linguistics and language in use will be able to benefit metaphor detection. Our hope is that this work opens a door to more diverse kinds of situational features to be used for metaphor detection, together with linguistically inspired features. In addition, our work reinforces and extends earlier insights into social and cognitive factors that influence usage of metaphor in discussion, and illustrates a new impact of accurate event extraction.

The remainder of the paper is organized as follows. Section 2 relates our work to prior work on computational metaphor detection. Section 3 describes the data used for our experiment. Section 4 explains the event extraction method we adopted. Section 5 illustrates popular metaphors related to cancer events in our data through a statistical analysis. Section 6 presents our successful metaphor disambiguation experiments. Section 7 concludes the paper with a discussion of limitations and next steps in the work.

2 Related Work

In this section, we introduce two main bodies of relevant prior work in language technologies: case studies in online medical support communities and computational metaphor detection.

2.1 Case Studies in Online Medical Support Communities

Analysis of language patterns in online cancer forums have shown effects of time and experience. For example, with respect to time, Nguyen and Rosé (2011) examine how language use patterns are linked with increased personal connection with the community over time. They show consistent growth in adoption of community language usage norms over time. Prior work on online cancer support discussion forums also shows that participants' behavior patterns are influenced by the experience of stress-inducing events. For example, Wen and Rosé (2012) show that frequency of participants' posting behavior is correlated with stress-inducing events. Wen et al. (2011) conducted a study to analyze patterns of discussion forum posts relating to one specific woman's cancer treatment process. However, these studies have not performed computational analysis on the role of metaphor in these tasks. Metaphor use in this domain is highly prevalent, and plays an important role in analysis of language use, however its usage patterns in this type of context have not been systematically explored.

2.2 Computational Metaphor Detection

There has been much work on computational metaphor detection. Among these published works, the approaches used have typically fallen into one of three categories: selectional preferences, abstractness and concreteness, and lexical incoherence.

Selectional preferences relate to how semantically compatible predicates are with particular arguments. For example, the verb *eat* prefers *food* as an object over *chair*. The idea of using selectional preferences for metaphor detection is that metaphorically used words tend to break selectional preferences. In the example of *The clouds sailed across the sky*, *sailed* is determined to be a metaphor since *clouds* as a subject violates its selectional preferences. Selectional preferences have been considered in a variety of studies about metaphor detection (Martin, 1996; Shutova and Teufel, 2010; Shutova et al., 2010; Shutova et al., 2013; Huang, 2014)

The abstractness/concreteness approach associates metaphorical use with the degree of abstractness and concreteness within the components of a phrase. In an phrase of adjective and noun such as *green idea* and *green frog*, the former is considered metaphorical since an abstract word (*idea*) is modified by a concrete word (*green*), while the latter is considered literal since both words are concrete (Turney et al., 2011). Broadwell et al. (2013) use measures of imageability to detect metaphor, a similar concept to abstractness and concreteness.

The lexical coherence approach uses the fact that metaphorically used words are semantically not coherent with context words. Broadwell et al. (2013) use topic chaining to categorize words as non-metaphorical when they have a semantic relationship to the main topic. Sporleder and Li (2009) also use lexical chains and semantic cohesion graphs to detect metaphors.

To the best of our knowledge, there has been no computational work on the effect of situational factors, such as the experience of stressful events, on computational metaphor detection. Demonstrating how situational factors could be useful for computational metaphor detection is one of our contributions.

3 Data

We conduct experiments using data from discussion boards for an online breast cancer support group. Participants in the discussion forums are mainly patients, family members, and caregivers. People use the discussion for exchanging both informational support and emotional support with each other by sharing their stories, and through questioning and answering. Some people begin participating in this forum immediately after being diagnosed with cancer, while others do not make their first post until a later event in the cancer treatment process, such as chemotherapy (Wen and Rosé, 2012).

The data contains all the public posts, users, and profiles on the discussion boards from October 2001 to January 2011. The dataset consists of 1,562,459 messages and 90,242 registered members. 31,307 users have at least one post, and the average number of posts per user is 24.

We picked this dataset for our study of relationship between metaphor and situational factors for two reasons. First, people in this community have a common set of events (e.g cancer diagnosis, chemotherapy, etc.) that are frequently discussed in user posts. Second, people use metaphorical expressions quite frequently in this domain. Thus, the dataset is suitable for a study about metaphor use related with user events. Below is an example post containing metaphors. Some parts in the post have been changed for private information.

> Meghan, I was diagnosed this pst 09/02/07. I was upset for a day when I realized after I had two mammograms and the ultrasound that I had cancer-I didn't have a diagnosis, but I knew. After the ultrasound came the biopsy and then the diagnosis, I was fine. I did research. I made up my mind about what treatement I thought I wanted. I was good...I really was fine up to my visit with the surgeon last week. That made it really real for me.

> I am waiting for my breast MRI results, and I have to have an ultrasound needle guided auxillary node biopsy before I even get to schedule my surgery. My PET showed other issues in the breast, thus the MRI and the biopsy. Be kind to yourself. It will be a *roller coaster ride* of emotions. Some days really up and strong, other days needing lots of hugs and kleenex. Melody

4 Extracting Cancer Event Histories

The cancer events investigated in this paper include *Diagnosis*, *Chemotherapy*, *Radiation Therapy*, *Lumpectomy*, *Mastectomy*, *Breast Reconstruction*, *Cancer Recurrence* and *Metastasis*. All these eight events induce significant physical, practical and emotional challenges. The event dates are extracted from the users' posts as well as the "Diagnosis" and "Biography" sections in their user profiles. 33% of members filled in a personal profile providing additional information about themselves and their disease (e.g., age, occupation, cancer stage, diagnosis date).

We apply the approach of Wen et al. (2013) to extract dates of cancer events for each of the users from their posting histories. A temporal tagger retrieves and normalizes dates mentioned informally in social media to actual month and year referents. Building on this, an event date extraction system learns to integrate the likelihood of candidate dates extracted from time-rich sentences with temporal constraints extracted from event-related sentences.

Wen et al. (2013) evaluate their event extraction approach in comparison with the best competing state-of-the-art approach and show that their approach performs significantly better, achieving an 88% F1 (corresponding to 91% precision and 85% recall) at resolution of extracted temporal expressions to actual calendar dates, and correctly identifies 90% of the event dates that are possible given the performance of that temporal extraction step.

We adopt the same method to extract all users' cancer event dates in our corpus. Note that even were we to use a perfect event extraction system, we can only extract events that the users explicitly mention in their posts. Users may experience additional events during their cancer treatment process, and simply choose not to mention them during their posts.

5 Investigation into the Connection between Metaphor and Events

As users continue to participate in the cancer community we are studying, over time they experience more and more significant cancer events. Earlier work (Wen and Rosé, 2012) shows elevated levels of participation frequency and posting frequency around the time of and immediately after experiencing one of these stress-causing events. This pattern suggests that one way users work to process their traumatic experience is by participating in the forum and obtaining support from other people who are going through similar experiences. Since using metaphorical language suggests elevated levels of cognitive effort related to the associated concept, it is reasonable to expect that users may also engage in a higher concentration of metaphorical language during this time as well as an additional reflection of that processing. In this section, we investigate how the use of metaphor changes with respect to specific traumatic cancer events. We examine a set of common metaphors to see whether situational factors, i.e. cancer events, affect their use. We use cancer event dates extracted in (Wen et al., 2013) as described in Section 4

5.1 Before and After Events

As our first analysis of the relationship between metaphor use and events, we pick eight unambiguous metaphor words in our data – *journey*, *boat*, *warrior*, *angel*, *battle*, *victor*, *one step at a time*, and *roller coaster ride* – and consider the distribution of these metaphors around each event. We categorized these metaphors as unambiguous based on their usage within a small sample of posts we analyzed by hand. Since these are unambiguous, we can be sure that each time we detect these words being used, the speaker is making a metaphor. For each metaphor-event pair, we construct a graph showcasing the frequency of the metaphor usage both before and after the event. We center each user's post dates around the month of the event, so times on the x-axis are relative dates rather than absolute dates (the center of the graph corresponds to the actual event month).

The graphs for *journey* and *warrior* paired with the diagnosis event are shown in Figure 1 and Figure 2, respectively.

Certain metaphor/event pairs show a peak around the event, or at 1 year after the event, for example on the anniversary of diagnosis, which is a significant event in the life of a cancer patient. However, the pattern does not hold across all such pairs, making it difficult to generalize. For example, in Figure 1, we see a peak of metaphor frequency occurring at the time of the event, but in Figure 2, we do not see such a peak at the time of the event, but see other peaks both before and after the event date. Another complicating factor is that different users experience different cancer treatment timelines. For instance, one user might experience these events over a long period of time, whereas another user may encounter these events in quick succession (Wen and Rosé, 2012). These factors motivated us to consider other methods, including hierarchical mixed models, for more in-depth analysis.

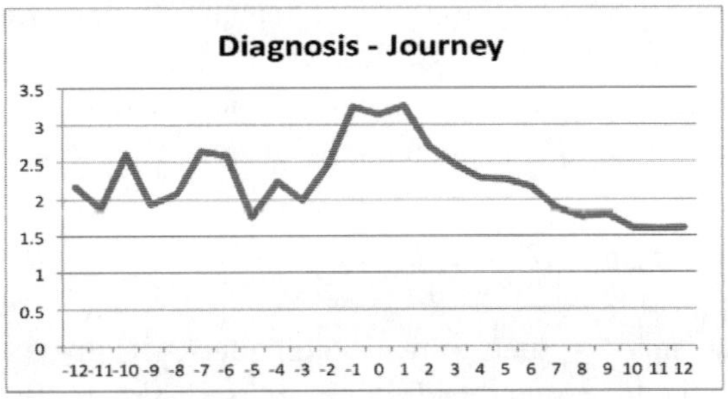

Figure 1: Distribution of *journey* metaphor centered around diagnosis event (x-axis: months from event, y-axis: average frequency of metaphor usage)

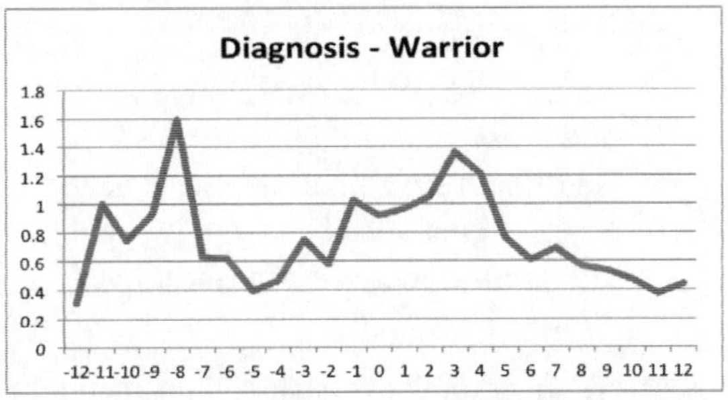

Figure 2: Distribution of *warrior* metaphor centered around diagnosis event (x-axis: months from event, y-axis: average frequency of metaphor usage)

5.2 Associated Events Analysis

Hierarchical mixed models enable us to model the effect of the experience of a cancer event in the history of a user while controlling for other important factors, such as time and personal tendency. We prepared data for analysis by sampling users. We identified the list of users who used any of our target metaphors at least once, and extracted all the posts of those users. In our models, we treat the message as the unit of analysis, and the dependent measure is always either the presence or absence of a specific metaphor, or the presence or absence of metaphorical language more generally, in all cases indicated by a dichotomous variable. Independent variables including dichotomous indicators of the experience of a specific cancer event in the recent past. We treat each user post as being in the critical period of a cancer event if the post date falls within a time window of two months prior to the event month to two months after the event month, which we selected based on informal observation. Data statistics are shown in Table 1.

We tested the association between each dependent variable and the set of independent variables. These hierarchical mixed models were built using the Generalized Linear Latent and Mixed Models (GLLAMM) add-on package in STATA (Rabe-Hesketh and Skrondal, 2008; Rabe-Hesketh et al., 2004), using maximum likelihood estimation to estimate the models. A random intercept is included for each poster, which is necessary for avoiding obtaining biased estimates of the parameters since there were multiple data points for each user, and users varied in their tendency to use metaphorical language or not. We also experimented with time as an independent variable to control for potential consistent increases in usage of metaphorical language over time, but we did not find any such strong effect, and so we dropped this variable from our models.

We did not find significant effects with a dependent measure that indicated that any of the set of metaphors were used, however, we did find significant associations between metaphors and events when we used dependent variables associated with specific metaphors. Our finding was that the subset of events associated with a metaphor varied by metaphor in a way that made sense given the conno-

metaphor	#		%	
	M	L	M	L
journey	5,787	1,329,560	0.43	99.57
boat	21,398	1,313,849	1.60	98.40
warrior	3,462	1,331,785	0.26	99.74
angel	16,025	1,319,222	1.20	98.80
battle	6,347	1,328,900	0.48	99.52
victor	3,540	1,331,707	0.27	99.73
one step at a time	1,554	1,333,693	0.12	99.88
roller coaster ride	536	1,334,711	0.04	99.96
all	64,755	1,270,492	4.85	95.15

Table 1: Corpus-wide unambiguous popular metaphor use statistics (among posts where the user used the metaphor at least once) (**M**: posts that contain each metaphor, **L**: posts that do not contain each metaphor).

candidate	associated events
journey	diagnosis, recurrence, mastectomy
boat	diagnosis, reconstruction
warrior	chemo
angel	chemo, rads, mets
battle	diagnosis, rads, lumpectomy
victor	chemo, rads, reconstruction
one step at a time	diagnosis
roller coaster ride	diagnosis, reconstruction

Table 2: Metaphor candidates and their associated events

tation of the metaphor. For instance, *warrior* is associated with chemo, and *journey* is associated with diagnosis, recurrence, and mastectomy. Associations for all metaphors used for analysis are listed in Table 2.

6 Metaphor Disambiguation

Knowing that there is a significant association between the experience of a cancer event and the usage of a metaphor opens up the possibility for using knowledge of a user's experience of cancer events in the interpretation of their language choices. In particular, if they use a word that may or may not be metaphorical, and the metaphorical usage is associated with a cancer event that occurred in their recent past, then the model should be more likely to predict the metaphorical interpretation. Conversely, if the user is not within the critical period of the event associated with the potential metaphorical interpretation, the metaphorical interpretation should be correspondingly less preferred. We hypothesize that usage of this contextual information might improve the accuracy of disambiguation of potentially metaphorical language. In this section, we test that hypothesis in a corpus based experiment conducted this time on a set of ambiguous, potentially metaphorical words.

6.1 Task

Our task is metaphor disambiguation: given a candidate word, decide whether the word is used metaphorically or literally in a post. For example, *road* in (1) is used metaphorically, and *road* in (2) is used literally. The task is to classify *road* into metaphor and literal use.

(1) Great hobbies! ... My hobbie that I love is *road* bike riding. My husband and I both have bikes and we love to ride. ... That's the beauty of living in the south is that you can ride all year long.

(2) Another thing to consider is cosmetic outcome. ... If you have a recurrence of cancer and have to do a mast down the *road*, reconstruction is more difficult after having radiation. ...

6.2 Data Annotation

We picked six metaphor candidates that appear either metaphorically or literally in the breastcancer corpus: *candle*, *light*, *ride*, *road*, *spice*, and *train*.

We employed MTurk workers to annotate metaphor use for candidate words. A candidate word was given highlighted in the full post it came from. MTurkers were instructed to copy and paste the sentence where a given highlighted word is contained to a given text box to make sure that MTurkers do not give a random answer. They were given a simple definition of metaphor from Wikipedia along with a few examples to guide them. Then, they were questioned whether the highlighted word is used metaphorically or literally. Each candidate word was labeled by five different MTurk workers, and we paid $0.03 for annotating each word. To control annotation quality, we required that all workers have a United States location and have 98% or more of their previous submissions accepted. We filtered out annotations whose the first task of copy and paste failed, and 18 out of 11,675 annotations were excluded.

To evaluate the reliability of the annotations by MTurkers, we calculated Fleiss's kappa (Fleiss, 1971). Fleiss's kappa is appropriate for assessing inter-reliability when different items are rated by different judges. The annotation was 1 if the MTurker coded a word as a metaphorical use, otherwise the annotation was 0. The kappa value is 0.80.

We split the data randomly into two subsets, one for analysis of related events, and the other for classification. The former set contains 803 instances, and the latter contains 1,532 instances. The unusual number of instances within each subset arises from the fact that some posts contain multiple metaphors, and we specifically chose to set aside 1,500 posts for classification.

6.3 Analysis on Associated Events

We performed a statistical analysis on the six metaphor candidate words as in Section 5.2. We combined the users from all the six metaphor candidates, and extracted posts of these users. Independent variables for the model were binary values for each event, where the value is 1 if a post was written in the critical period (defined previously in Section 5.2), and 0 otherwise. The dependent variable is a binary value regarding the usage of a metaphor candidate within a post. If a particular post does not include a metaphor candidate or if a post includes a literally used metaphor candidate, the binary dependent value is set to 0. Otherwise, it is set to 1.

candidate	#		%	
	N	**L**	**N**	**L**
candle*	4	18	18.18	81.81
light	503	179	73.75	26.25
ride	234	185	55.85	44.15
road	924	129	87.75	12.25
spice*	3	21	12.50	87.50
train	94	41	69.63	30.37
all	1762	573	75.46	24.54

Table 3: Metaphor use statistics of data used for MTurk (* indicates metaphor candidates for which the literal usage is more common than the non-literal one, **N**: nonliteral use **L**: literal use).

candidate	**associated events**
candle	none
light	diagnosis, rads, mast
ride	diagnosis
road	diagnosis, rads
spice	none
train	mast

Table 4: Metaphor candidates and their associated events

The results of conducting the hierarchical mixed model analysis on the data similar to the one conducted above on non-ambiguous metaphors suggest that some candidate words show an association with different cancer events as shown in Table 4.

6.4 Classification

We used the LightSIDE (Mayfield and Penstein-Rosé, 2010) toolkit for extracting features and classification. For the machine learning algorithm, we used the support vector machine (SVM) classifier provided in LightSIDE with the default options. We used basic unigram features extracted by LightSIDE.

To see the effect of event information for classification, we defined two sets of event features. One is a feature vector over all the events, consisting of

model	Accuracy	Kappa	Precision	Recall	F1 score
(1) word	0.8133	0.3493	0.8105	0.9827	0.8884
(2) context unigram	0.8094	0.4701	0.8651	0.8860	0.8754
(3) context unigram + event	0.8127	0.4777	0.8657	0.8903	0.8778
(4) context unigram + associated event	0.8146	0.4729	0.8612	0.8998	0.8801
(5) context unigram + fs	0.8277	0.5155	0.8731	0.9033	0.8879
(6) **context unigram + event + fs**	**0.8336**	**0.5325**	**0.8772**	**0.9067**	**0.8917**
(7) context unigram + associated event + fs	0.8244	0.504	0.8695	0.9033	0.8861

Table 5: Performance on metaphor disambiguation evaluation. (6) is significantly better than (5) [p=0.013] (fs.: used feature selection)

both binary variables to indicate whether or not a post belongs to the critical period of each event, and numerical variables to indicate how many months the post is written from a known event. We will refer to these features as *event* in Table 5. The other is a binary variable to indicate whether or not a post belongs to the critical period of *any* of the associated events for the given metaphor (defined in Section 6.3). We will refer to this feature as *associated event* in Table 5.

We used multilevel modeling for the features when including *associated event*. We also used the FeatureSelection feature in LightSIDE, where a subset of features is picked on each fold before passing it to the learning plugin. We performed 10-fold cross validation for these experiments.

Because we want to see the effect of event information, we compare our model with a unigram model that uses only the word itself as in (Klebanov et al., 2014), and the context unigram model which uses all the context words in a post as features as baselines.

6.5 Results

Table 5 displays the results for our experiments. First, we observe the strong performance of the unigram baseline. As in (Klebanov et al., 2014), our evaluation also shows that just using the word currently being classified gives relatively high performance. This result suggests that our candidate words are popular metaphors repeatedly used metaphorically in this domain, as precision is above 80%.

Second, surprisingly, we do not see improvement on accuracy from adding the context words as features. However, we do observe that this addition results in a higher kappa value than just using the candidate words themselves.

Finally, we can see both *event* and *associated event* features show promising results. Both additions give higher result when added to the context unigram model, and the *event* features continue to show improvement when considering models with feature selection. The best model, using *event* features with feature selection, shows significant improvement ($p < 0.05$) over the next best model of context unigram with feature selection.

7 Conclusion

In this paper, we discussed how situational factors affect people's metaphor use. We presented a study in an online medical support community, which contains a variety of related events (e.g. diagnosis, chemotherapy, etc.). First, we investigated how popular unambiguous metaphors in the discussion forum are used in relation to major cancer events. Second, we demonstrated that event information can be helpful for a computational metaphor disambiguation task over ambiguous candidate metaphor words. In this work we quantitatively verified the effect of situational features.

Our analysis showed that some popular unambiguous metaphors in the discussion forum are used in connection with stressful cancer events. Usage of different metaphors is associated with different cancer events. We also observed that the personal tendency factor is about 10 times as strong as the situational factor. For our future work, it will be an interesting problem to design a model considering the personal tendency factor. It will require a latent variable model to properly tease these factors apart.

In addition, our metaphor disambiguation experiments validated the proposed association between cancer events and metaphor usage. Using event information as features showed significant improvement. Although our classification results using associated event information show weak improvement to no improvement depending on whether feature selection is used, it is important to note that our analysis consistently identified a strong relationship between metaphors and their associated events (Table 4). Therefore, we believe that it is crucial to develop a classification model that can better leverage the metaphor-event association, which remains as our future work. We also want to try different sized context windows for the critical period of a cancer event in order to see the effect of time with respect to situational factors.

One limitation of this research is that our analysis relies on the event extraction results. Although the event extraction approach we adopted is currently the best performing state-of-the-art technique, it still makes mistakes that could make our analysis inaccurate. Another limitation is that it is hard to obtain data big enough to split the data into subparts for both the hierarchical mixed model analysis and classification.

Acknowledgments

This research was supported in part by NSF Grant IIS-1302522.

References

George Aaron Broadwell, Umit Boz, Ignacio Cases, Tomek Strzalkowski, Laurie Feldman, Sarah Taylor, Samira Shaikh, Ting Liu, Kit Cho, and Nick Webb. 2013. Using imageability and topic chaining to locate metaphors in linguistic corpora. In *Social Computing, Behavioral-Cultural Modeling and Prediction*, pages 102–110. Springer.

Joseph L Fleiss. 1971. Measuring nominal scale agreement among many raters. *Psychological bulletin*, 76(5):378–382.

Ting-Hao Kenneth Huang. 2014. Social metaphor detection via topical analysis. In *Sixth International Joint Conference on Natural Language Processing*, page 14.

Hyeju Jang, Mario Piergallini, Miaomiao Wen, and Carolyn Penstein Rosé. 2014. Conversational metaphors in use: Exploring the contrast between technical and everyday notions of metaphor. *ACL 2014*, page 1.

Beata Beigman Klebanov, Chee Wee Leong, Michael Heilman, and Michael Flor. 2014. Different texts, same metaphors: Unigrams and beyond. *ACL 2014*, page 11.

James H Martin. 1996. Computational approaches to figurative language. *Metaphor and Symbol*, 11(1):85–100.

Elijah Mayfield and Carolyn Penstein-Rosé. 2010. An interactive tool for supporting error analysis for text mining. In *Proceedings of the NAACL HLT 2010 Demonstration Session*, pages 25–28. Association for Computational Linguistics.

Dong Nguyen and Carolyn P Rosé. 2011. Language use as a reflection of socialization in online communities. In *Proceedings of the Workshop on Languages in Social Media*, pages 76–85. Association for Computational Linguistics.

Sophia Rabe-Hesketh and Anders Skrondal. 2008. *Multilevel and longitudinal modeling using Stata*. STATA press.

Sophia Rabe-Hesketh, Anders Skrondal, and Andrew Pickles. 2004. Gllamm manual.

SL. David Ritchie. 2013. *Metaphor (Key Topics in Semantics and Pragmatics)*. Cambridge university press.

Ekaterina Shutova and Simone Teufel. 2010. Metaphor corpus annotated for source-target domain mappings. In *LREC*.

Ekaterina Shutova, Lin Sun, and Anna Korhonen. 2010. Metaphor identification using verb and noun clustering. In *Proceedings of the 23rd International Conference on Computational Linguistics*, pages 1002–1010. Association for Computational Linguistics.

Ekaterina Shutova, Simone Teufel, and Anna Korhonen. 2013. Statistical metaphor processing. *Computational Linguistics*, 39(2):301–353.

Caroline Sporleder and Linlin Li. 2009. Unsupervised recognition of literal and non-literal use of idiomatic expressions. In *Proceedings of the 12th Conference of the European Chapter of the Association for Computational Linguistics*, pages 754–762. Association for Computational Linguistics.

Peter D Turney, Yair Neuman, Dan Assaf, and Yohai Cohen. 2011. Literal and metaphorical sense identification through concrete and abstract context. In *Proceedings of the 2011 Conference on the Empirical Methods in Natural Language Processing*, pages 680–690.

Miaomiao Wen and Carolyn Penstein Rosé. 2012. Understanding participant behavior trajectories in online health support groups using automatic extraction methods. In *Proceedings of the 17th ACM international conference on Supporting group work*, pages 179–188. ACM.

Kuang-Yi Wen, Fiona McTavish, Gary Kreps, Meg Wise, and David Gustafson. 2011. From diagnosis to death: A case study of coping with breast cancer as seen through online discussion group messages. *Journal of Computer-Mediated Communication*, 16(2):331–361.

Miaomiao Wen, Zeyu Zheng, Hyeju Jang, Guang Xiang, and Carolyn Penstein Rosé. 2013. Extracting events with informal temporal references in personal histories in online communities. In *ACL (2)*, pages 836–842.

Supervised Word-Level Metaphor Detection: Experiments with Concreteness and Reweighting of Examples

Beata Beigman Klebanov, Chee Wee Leong, and Michael Flor
Educational Testing Service
660 Rosedale Road
Princeton, NJ 08541
bbeigmanklebanov,cleong,mflor@ets.org

Abstract

We present a supervised machine learning system for word-level classification of all content words in a running text as being metaphorical or non-metaphorical. The system provides a substantial improvement upon a previously published baseline, using re-weighting of the training examples and using features derived from a concreteness database. We observe that while the first manipulation was very effective, the second was only slightly so. Possible reasons for these observations are discussed.

1 Introduction

In this paper, we present a set of experiments aimed at improving on previous work on the task of supervised word-level detection of linguistic metaphor in running text. The use of supervised machine learning techniques for metaphor identification has increased manyfold in the recent years (see section 10, Related Work, for a review and references), partially due to the availability of large-scale annotated resources for training and evaluating the algorithms, such as the VU Amsterdam corpus (Steen et al., 2010), datasets built as part of a U.S. government-funded initiative to advance the state-of-art in metaphor identification and interpretation (Mohler et al., 2013; Strzalkowski et al., 2013), and recent annotation efforts with other kinds of data (Beigman Klebanov and Flor, 2013; Jang et al., 2014). Some of these data are publicly available (Steen et al., 2010), allowing for benchmarking and for measuring incremental improvements, which is the approach taken in this paper.

Data	#Texts	content tokens	% metaphors
News	49	18,519	18%
Fiction	11	17,836	14%
Academic	12	29,469	13%
Conversation	18	15,667	7%
Essay Set A	85	21,838	11%
Essay Set B	79	22,662	12 %

Table 1: The sizes of the datasets used in this study, and the proportion of metaphors. Content tokens are nouns, adjectives, adverbs, and verbs.

We start with a baseline set of features and training regime from Beigman Klebanov et al. (2014), and investigate the impact of re-weighting of training examples and of a suite of features related to concreteness of the target concept, as well as to the difference in concreteness within certain types of dependency relations. The usage of concreteness features was previously discussed in the literature; to our knowledge, these features have not yet been evaluated for their impact in a comprehensive system for word-level metaphor detection, apart from the concreteness features as used in Beigman Klebanov et al. (2014), which we use as a baseline.

2 Data

2.1 VU Amsterdam Data

We use the VU Amsterdam metaphor-annotated dataset.[1] The dataset consists of fragments sampled across four genres from the British National

[1] http://www2.let.vu.nl/oz/metaphorlab/metcor/search/index.html

Proceedings of the Third Workshop on Metaphor in NLP, pages 11–20,
Denver, Colorado, June 5, 2015.

Corpus (BNC): Academic, News, Conversation, and Fiction. The data is annotated according to the MIPVU procedure (Steen et al., 2010) with the inter-annotator reliability of $\kappa > 0.8$.

In order to allow for direct comparison with prior work, we used the same subset of these data as Beigman Klebanov et al. (2014), in the same cross-validation setting. The total of 90 fragments are used in cross-validation: 10-fold on News, 9-fold on Conversation, 11 on Fiction, and 12 on Academic. All instances from the same text were always placed in the same fold. Table 1 shows the sizes of the datasets for each genre, as well as the proportion of metaphors therein.

2.2 Essay Data

The dataset contains 174 essays written for a large-scale college-level assessment of analytical writing. The essays were written in response to one of the following two topics: Discuss the statement "High-speed electronic communications media, such as electronic mail and television, tend to prevent meaningful and thoughtful communication" (Set A, 85 essays), and "In the age of television, reading books is not as important as it once was. People can learn as much by watching television as they can by reading books." (Set B, 79 essays). These essays were annotated for argumentation-relevant metaphors (Beigman Klebanov and Flor, 2013), with inter-annotator reliability of κ = 0.58 and κ = 0.56 for Set A and Set B, respectively. We will report results for 10-fold cross-validation on each of sets A and B, as well as across prompts, where the machine learner would be trained on Set A and tested on Set B and vice versa. Please refer to Table 1 for further details about the datasets. This dataset was used in Beigman Klebanov et al. (2014), allowing for a direct comparison.

3 Experimental Set-Up

In this study, each content-word token in a text is an instance that is classified as either a metaphor or not a metaphor. We use the logistic regression classifier as implemented in the SKLL package (Blanchard et al., 2013), which is based on scikit-learn (Pedregosa et al., 2011), with F1 optimization ("metaphor" class). Performance will be evaluated using Precision, Recall, and F-1 score, for the positive ("metaphor") class.

As a baseline, we use the best performing feature set from Beigman Klebanov et al. (2014), who investigated supervised word-level identification of metaphors. We investigate the effect of reweighting of examples, as well as the effectiveness of features related to the notion of concreteness.

4 Baseline System

As a baseline, we use the best feature set from Beigman Klebanov et al. (2014). Specifically, the baseline contains the following families of features:

- Unigrams;
- Part-of-speech tags generated by Stanford POS tagger 3.3.0 (Toutanova et al., 2003);
- Mean concreteness values from Brysbaert et al. (2013) set of concreteness norms, represented using 0.25-wide bins that span the 1-5 range of possible values;
- $log\frac{P(w|t)}{P(w)}$ values for each of 100 topics generated by Latent Dirichlet Allocation (Blei et al., 2003) from the NYT corpus (Sandhaus, 2008).

5 Experiment 1: Re-weighting of Examples

Given that the category distribution is generally heavily skewed towards the non-metaphor category (see Table 1), we experimented with cost-sensitive machine learning techniques to try to correct for the imbalanced class distribution (Yang et al., 2014; Muller et al., 2014). The first technique uses **AutoWeight** (as implemented in the *auto* flag in scikit-learn toolkit), where we assign weights that are inversely proportional to the class frequencies.[2] Table 2 shows the results.

The effect of auto-weighting on the VUA data is quite dramatic: A 14-point drop in precision is offset by a 32-point increase in recall, on average, along with a 10-point average increase in F1 score. The precision-recall balance for VUA data changed from P=0.58, R=0.34 to P=0.44, R=0.66, nearly doubling

[2]The re-weighting of examples was only applied to training data; the test data is unweighted.

Data	Baseline			AutoWeighting		
	P	R	F	P	R	F
A-B	.71	.35	.47	.52	.71	.60
B-A	.57	.49	.53	.40	.67	.50
Set A	.70	.48	.57	.50	.75	.60
Set B	.76	.59	.67	.57	.80	.67
Av. Essays	.69	.48	.56	.50	.74	.59
Acad.	.63	.35	.42	.53	.66	.56
Conv.	.50	.24	.32	.29	.69	.39
Fiction	.55	.29	.38	.41	.61	.49
News	.64	.46	.54	.53	.68	.59
Av. VUA	.58	.34	.41	.44	.66	.51

Table 2: Performance of a model with AutoWeighted training examples in comparison to the unweighted baseline, in terms of Precision (P), Recall (R), and F-1 score (F) for the positive ("metaphor") class. A-B and B-A correspond to training-testing scenarios where the system is trained on Set A and tested on Set B and vice versa, respectively. All other figures report average performance across the cross-validation folds.

the recall. The effect on essay data is such that the average drop in precision is larger than for VUA data (19 points) while the improvement in recall is smaller (26 points). The average increase in F-1 score is about 3 points, with the maximum of up to 13 F-1 points (A-B evaluation) and a 3-point drop for B-A evaluation.

Overall, this experiment shows that the feature set can support a radical change in the balance between precision and recall. When precision is a priority (as in a situation where feedback to the user is provided in the form of highlighting of the metaphorically used words, for example), it is possible to achieve nearly 70% precision, while recovering about half the metaphors. When recall is a priority (possibly when an overall per-essay metaphoricity rate is estimated and used as a feature in an essay scoring system), it is possible to recover about 3 out of every 4 metaphors, with about 50% precision. For VUA data, a similar trend is observed, with somewhat worse performance, on average, than on essay data. The performance on the VUA News and Academic data is in line with the findings for the cross-prompt generalization in the essay data, whereas Conversation and Fiction genres are more difficult for the current system.[3]

Having observed the results of the auto-weighting experiments, we conjectured that perhaps a more even balance of precision and recall can be obtained if the re-weighting gives extra weight to "metaphor" class, but not to the extent that the auto-weighting scheme does. In the second experiment, we tune the weight parameter using grid search on the training data (through a secondary 3-fold cross-validation within training data) to find the optimal weighting in terms of F-score (**OptiWeight**); the best-performing weight was then evaluated on the test data (for cross-prompt evaluations) or the test fold (cross-validations). We used the grid from 1:1 weighting up to 8:1, with increments of 0.33.

The first finding of note is that the optimal weighting for the "metaphor" class is lower than the auto-weight. For example, given that metaphors constitute 11-12% of instances in the essay data, the auto-weighting scheme for the A-B and B-A evaluations would choose the weights to be about 8:1, whereas the grid search settled on 3:1 when trained on prompt A and 3.33:1 when trained on prompt B. A similar observation pertains to the VUA data: The auto-weighting is expected to be about 4.5:1 for News data, yet the grid search settled on 4:1, on average across folds. These observations suggest that the auto-weighting scheme might not be the optimal re-weighting strategy when optimizing for F1 score with equal importance of precision and recall.

Table 3 shows the performance of the optimized weighting scheme. For VUA data, the changes in performance are generally positive albeit slight – the F1 score increases by one point for 3 out of 4 evaluations). For essay data, it is clear that the imbalance between precision and recall is substantially reduced (from the average difference between recall and precision of 0.24 for the auto-weighted scheme to the average difference of 0.08 for the optimized weights; see column *D* in the Table). The best effect was observed for the B-A evaluation (train on set B, test on set A) – a 6-point increase in preci-

[3]This could be partially explained by the fact that the samples for Fiction and Conversation contain long excerpts from the same text, so they allow for less diversity than samples in the News set, with a larger number of shorter excerpts, although performance on the Academic set is not quite in line with these observations.

Data	AutoWeight				OptiWeight			
	P	R	F	*D*	P	R	F	*D*
A-B	.52	.71	.60	*.19*	.58	.55	.57	*-.03*
B-A	.40	.67	.50	*.27*	.46	.65	.54	*.20*
A	.50	.75	.60	*.25*	.56	.66	.60	*.11*
B	.57	.80	.67	*.23*	.52	.69	.68	*.03*
Av.	.50	.74	.59	*.24*	.57	.64	.60	*.08*
Ac.	.53	.66	.56	*.14*	.52	.69	.57	*.17*
Con.	.29	.69	.39	*.39*	.32	.63	.40	*.31*
Fict.	.41	.61	.49	*.20*	.40	.66	.49	*.26*
News	.53	.68	.59	*.15*	.51	.71	.60	*.20*
Av.	.44	.66	.51	*.22*	44	.67	.51	*.24*

Table 3: Performance of a model with optimally weighted training examples in comparison to the auto-weighted scheme, in terms of Precision (P), Recall (R), F-1 score (F), and the difference between Recall and Precision (D). A-B and B-A correspond to training-testing scenarios where the system is trained on Set A and tested on Set B and vice versa, respectively. All other figures report average performance across the cross-validation folds.

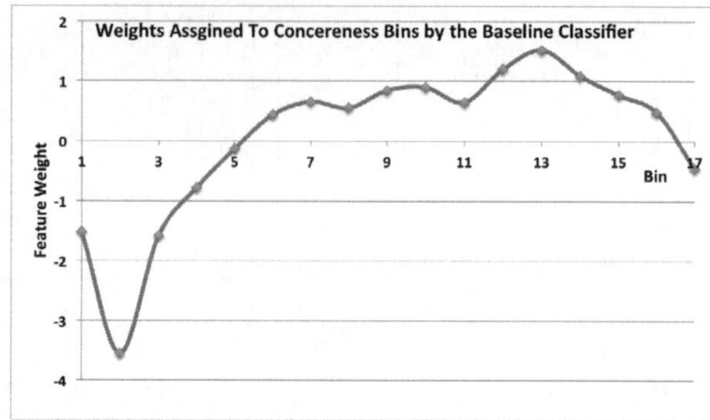

Figure 1: Weights assigned to the different concreteness bins by the logistic regression classifier with the baseline feature set in an unweighted training regime. The bins span the 1-5 range with 0.25 increments; words falling in bin 1 are the most abstract, while words falling in bin 17 are the most concrete.

sion compensated well for the 2-point drop in recall, relative to the auto-weighting scheme, with a resulting 4-point increase in F-score. The worst effect was observed for the A-B evaluation, where the increase of 6 points in precision was offset by a 16-point drop in recall. We conclude, therefore, that a grid-based optimization of weighting can help improve the precision-recall balance of the learning system and also improve the overall score in some cases.

6 Experiment 2: Re-representing concreteness information

In this paper, we use mean concreteness scores for words as published in the large-scale norming study by Brysbaert et al. (2013). The dataset has a reasonable coverage for our data; thus, 78% of tokens in Set A have a concreteness rating. The ratings are real numbers on the scale of 1 through 5; for example, *essentialness* has the concreteness of 1.04, while *sled* has the concreteness of 5.

The representation used by the baseline system bins the continuous values into 17 bins, starting with 1 and incrementing by 0.25 (the topmost bin has words with concreteness value of 5). Compared to a representation using a single continuous variable, the binned representation allows the machine-learner to provide different weights to different bins, thus modeling a non-linear relationship between concreteness and metaphoricity. Indeed, the logistic regression classifier has made precisely such use of this representation; Figure 1 shows the weights assigned by the classifier to the various bins, in a baseline model with unweighted examples trained on Set A data. Specifically, it is clear that abstract words receive a negative weight (predict the class "non-metaphor"), while concreteness values above 2.5 generally receive a positive weight (apart form the top bin, which happens to have only a single word in it).

One potential problem with binning as above is that some of the features become quite sparse; sparseness, in turn, makes them vulnerable to overfitting. Since the relationship between concreteness and feature weight is mostly monotonic (between bins 2 and 13), we experimented with defining bins that would encode various thresholds. Thus, bin $b5 = [2, 2.5]$ would fire whenever the value of the instance is at least 2 ($x \in [2, 5]$) or whenever the value of the instance is at most 2.5 ($x \in [1, 2.5]$); we call these theshold-up and threshold-down, respectively. Thus, instead of a set of 17 binary bins coding for intervals, we now have a set of 34 binary bins coding for upward and downward thresholds. The effect of this manipulation on the performance was generally small, yet this version of the concreteness feature yielded more robust performance. Specifically, the finding above of a drop in A-B performance in the optimal-weighting scheme is now largely mitigated, with precision staying the same (0.58), while recall improving from 0.55 to 0.60, and the resulting F1 score going up from 0.57 to 0.59, just one point below the auto-weighted version. The improved performance on B-A is preserved and even further improved, with P=0.50, R=0.62, F=0.55. For the rest of the datasets and weighting regimes, the performance was within one F-score point of the performance of the baseline feature set.

7 Experiment 3: Features capturing difference in concreteness

In this section, we present results of experiments trying to incorporate contextual information about the difference in concreteness between the adjective and its head noun (**AdjN**) and between the verb and its direct object (**VN**). The intuition behind this approach is that a metaphor is often used to describe an abstract concept in more familiar, physical terms. A concrete adjective modifying an abstract noun is likely to be used metaphorically (as in *soft revolution* or *dark thought*); similarly, a concrete verb with an abstract direct object is likely to be a metaphor (as in *pour consolation* or *drive innovation*). Turney et al. (2011) introduced a method for acquiring estimates of concreteness of words automatically, and measuring difference in concreteness in AdjN and VN constructions. They reported improved metaphor classification accuracies on constructed sets of AdjN and VN pairs.

We implemented a difference-in-concreteness feature using the values from Brysbaert et al. (2013) database. We parsed texts using Stanford Dependency Parser (de Marneffe et al., 2006), and identified all instances of amod, dobj, and rcmod relations that connect an adjective to a noun (amod), a verb to its direct object (dobj), and a verb in a relative clause to its head noun (rcmod). For example, in the sentence "I read the wonderful book that you recommended," the following pairs would be extracted: *wonderful-book* (amod), *read-book* (dobj), and *recommended-book* (rcmod). The difference-in-concreteness features are calculated for the adjectives and the verbs participating in the above constructions, as follows. Let (adj,n) be a pair of words in the amod relation; then the value of the difference in concreteness (DC) for the adjective is given by:

$$DC(adj) = Concr(adj) - Concr(n) \quad (1)$$

DC(v) for pairs (v,n) in dobj or rcmod relations is defined analogously. Features based on DC apply only to adjectives and verbs participating in the eligible constructions specified above.

To represent the difference in concreteness information for the machine learner, we utilize the binned thresholded representation introduced in section 6. The range of the values is now [-4,4]; hence we define 33 bins for each of the threshold-up and threshold-down versions.

Data	UPT+ CUpDown			UPT+ CUpDown+ DCUpDown		
	P	R	F	P	R	F
A-B	.712	.355	.474	.712	.362	.480
B-A	.563	.495	.527	.565	.494	.527
Set A	.703	.478	.567	.699	.475	.564
Set B	.757	.594	.665	.760	.604	.672
Av.	.684	.481	.558	.684	.484	.561
Acad.	.633	.350	.419	.636	.356	.425
Conv.	.500	.242	.317	.487	.236	.309
Fiction	.550	.291	.377	.559	.309	.395
News	.640	.465	.536	.636	.466	.536
Av.	.581	.337	.412	.580	.342	.416

Table 4: Performance of a model trained with unweighted examples with and without DC (difference in concreteness) features.

Table 4 shows the incremental improvement as a result of adding the DCUpDown features to the system with UPT+CUpDown. The improvement in recall and in F-score is very small – up to 0.4 F1 points on average across the evaluations. The largest increase in performance is observed for the VUA Fiction data (1.8 F1 points), with increases in both precision and recall. Since unweighted training scenario generally leads to high-precision low-recall models, an improvement in recall without drop in precision is helping the system to achieve a more balanced performance.

Table 5 shows the incremental improvements in performance when the system is trained in the auto-

Data	UPT+ CUpDown			UPT+ CUpDown+ DCUpDown		
	P	R	F	P	R	F
A-B	.521	.716	.603	.528	.713	.607
B-A	.401	.672	.503	.415	.670	.513
Set A	.499	.751	.597	.500	.747	.597
Set B	.571	.792	.663	.592	.773	.669
Av.	.498	.733	.592	.509	.726	.597
Acad.	.525	.662	.564	.525	.657	.562
Conv.	.292	.691	.393	.293	.691	.396
Fiction	.408	.608	.485	.411	.607	.486
News	.528	.674	.590	.530	.673	.590
Av.	.438	.659	.508	.440	.657	.509

Table 5: Performance of a model trained with auto-weighted examples with and without DC (difference in concreteness) features.

Data	UPT+ CUpDown			UPT+ CUpDown+ DCUpDown		
	P	R	F	P	R	F
A-B	.584	.596	.590	.593	.556	.574
B-A	.499	.620	.553	.485	.635	.550
Set A	.562	.659	.603	.561	.661	.604
Set B	.674	.697	.684	.662	.722	.690
Av.	.580	.643	.608	.575	.644	.605
Acad.	.532	.655	.564	.531	.655	.564
Conv.	.292	.691	.393	.293	.691	.396
Fiction	.400	.643	.490	.414	.621	.493
News	.513	.711	.592	.513	.709	.590
Av.	.434	.675	.510	.438	.669	.511

Table 6: Performance of a model trained with optimally-weighted examples with and without DC (difference in concreteness) features.

weighting regime. Here the effect of the difference in concreteness features is somewhat more pronounced for the essay data, with an average F1-score increase of 0.5 points, due to a 1.1 point average increase in precision along with 0.6-point drop in recall. Since auto-weighting generally leads to high-recall low-precision performance, improvement in precision is helping the system to achieve a more balanced performance.

The effect of the difference in concreteness features on the performance in the optimized weighting regime (Table 6) is less consistent across datasets; while we observe an improvement in precision in VUA data, the precision has dropped in the essay data, and vice versa with recall.

8 Results

In this section, we put together the different elements addressed in this paper, namely, the weighting regime, the different representation given to the concreteness feature relative to baseline, and the newly introduced difference in concreteness features. We compare performance to the baseline feature set (UPT+CBins) containing unigrams, POS features, topic features, and binned concreteness features (without thresholding), in an unweighted training regime, corresponding to the best feature set in Beigman Klebanov et al. (2014). These results are compared to the current best feature set (UPT+CUpDown+DCUpDown), in the optimized weighted training regime. The results are summarized in Table 7.

The overall effect of the proposed improvements is an absolute increase of 5.2 F1 points (9% relative increase) on essay data, on average, and 9.8 F1 points (24% relative increase) on VU Amsterdam data, on average.

9 Discussion

While the proposed improvements are effective overall, as shown in section 8 (Results), it is clear that the main driver of the improvement is the reweighting of examples, while the contribution of the other changes is very small (observe the small difference between the second column in Table 7 and the OptiWeight column in Table 3). The small improvement is perhaps not surprising, since the baseline model itself already contains a version of the concreteness features. Given the relevant literature that has put forward concreteness and difference in concreteness as important predictors of metaphoricity (Dunn, 2014; Tsvetkov et al., 2014; Gandy et al., 2013; Assaf et al., 2013; Turney et al., 2011), it is instructive to evaluate the overall contribution of the concreteness features over the UPT baseline (no concreteness features), across the different weighting regimes. Table 9 provides this information. The improvement afforded by the concreteness and

Data	UPT+ CBins unweighted (Baseline)			UPT+ CUpDown+ DCUpDown opti-weighted		
	P	R	F	P	R	F
A-B	.713	.351	.470	.593	.556	.574
B-A	.567	.491	.527	.485	.635	.550
Set A	.701	.478	.566	.561	.661	.604
Set B	.760	.592	.665	.662	.722	.690
Av.	.685	.478	.557	.575	.644	.605
Acad.	.631	.351	.419	.531	.655	.564
Conv.	.503	.241	.317	.293	.691	.396
Fiction	.551	.291	.378	.414	.621	.493
News	.640	.464	.536	.513	.709	.590
Av.	.581	.337	.413	.438	.669	.511

Table 7: Performance the baseline model UPT+CBins in the baseline configuration (unweighted) the UPT+CUpDown+DCUpDown model in opti-weighted configuration.

difference-in-concrteness features is 1.4 F1 points, on average, for the unweighted and auto-weighted regimes for essay data and 0.6 F1 points, on average, for the VUA data; there is virtually no improvement in the optimized weighting regime.

To exemplify the workings of the concreteness and difference-in-concreteness features, Table 8 shows the instances of the adjective *full* observed in Set B where UPT predicts non-metaphor (P(metaphor)=0.41), while the UPT+CUpDown+DCUpDown model predicts metaphoricity (P(metaphor) > 0.5). We use logistic regression models trained on Set A data to output the probabilities for class 1 (metaphor) for these instances. The metaphoricity prediction in these cases is mostly correct; the one instance where the prediction is incorrect seems to be due to noise in the human annotations: The instance where the system is most confident in assigning class 1 label – *full* in " full educational experience" – has the adjective *full* labeled as a non-metaphor, which appears to be an annotator error.

In light of the findings in the literature regarding the effectiveness of concreteness and of difference in concreteness for predicting metaphoricity, it is perhaps surprising that the effect of these features is rather modest.

Expression	Conc. Adj	Conc. N	P(meta)
full educational [experience]	3.6	1.8	0.72
reach FULL [potential]	3.6	1.9	0.60
to its FULL [potential]	3.6	1.9	0.60
FULL [understanding]	3.6	1.9	0.60
FULL [truth]	3.6	2.0	0.60

Table 8: Instances of the adjective *full* in Set B that are predicted to be non-metaphors by the UPT model trained on Set A in the unweighted regime, while the UPT+CUpDown+DCUpDown model classifies these as metaphors. The noun that is recognized as being in the amod relation with *full* is shown in square brackets. FULL (small caps) indicates an instance that is annotated as a metaphor; lowercase version corresponds to a non-metaphor annotation.

The incompleteness of the coverage of the concreteness database is one possible reason; 22% of instances in Set A do not have a concreteness value in the Brysbaert et al. (2013) database. Another possibility is that much of the information contained in concreteness features pertains to commonly used adjectives and verbs, which are covered by the unigram features. Mistakes made by the dependency parser in identifying eligible constructions could also impair effectiveness.

It is also possible that the concreteness ratings for adjectives in Brysbaert et al. (2013) data are somewhat problematic. In particular, we noticed that some adjectives that would seem quite concrete to us are given a concreteness rating that is not very high. For example, *round, white, soft, cold, rough, thin, dry, black, blue, hard, high, gray, heavy, deep, tall, ugly, small, strong, tiny, wide* all have a concreteness rating below 4 on a scale of 1 to 5. At the same time, they all have a fairly high value for the standard deviation (1.2-1.7) across about 30 responses collected per word. This suggests that when thinking about the concreteness of a word out of context, people might have conjured different senses, including metaphorical ones, and the judgment of concreteness in many of these cases might have been influenced by the metaphorical use. For example, if a person considered a concept like "dark thoughts" when assigning a concreteness value to *dark*, the concept is quite abstract, so perhaps the word *dark* is given a relatively abstract rating. This is, of course, circular, because the perceived abstractness of "dark thoughts" came about precisely because a concrete term *dark* is accommodated, metaphorically, into an abstract domain of thinking.

Another possibility is that it is not concreteness but some other property of adjectives that is relevant for metaphoricity. According to Hill and Korhonen (2014), the property of interest for adjectives is subjectivity, rather than concreteness. A feature capturing subjectivity of an adjective is a possible avenue for future work. In addition, they provide evidence that a potentially better way to quantify the concreteness of an adjective is to use mean concreteness of the nouns it modifies – as if concreteness for adjectives were a reflected property, based on its companion nouns. A large discrepancy between thusly calculated concreteness and the concreteness of the actual noun corresponds to non-literal meanings, especially for cases where the predicted concreteness of the adjective is high while the concreteness of the actual noun is low.

10 Related Work

The field of automated identification of metaphor has grown dramatically over the last few years, and there exists a plurality of approaches to the task. Shutova and Sun (2013) and Shutova et al. (2013) explored unsupervised clustering-based approaches. Features used in supervised learning approaches include selectional preferences violation, outlier detection, semantic analysis using topical signatures and ontologies, as well as n-gram features, among others (Tsvetkov et al., 2014; Schulder and Hovy, 2014; Beigman Klebanov et al., 2014; Mohler et al., 2013; Dunn, 2013; Tsvetkov et al., 2013; Hovy et al., 2013; Strzalkowski et al., 2013; Bethard et al., 2009; Pasanek and Sculley, 2008).

A number of previous studies used features capturing concreteness of concepts and difference in concreteness between concepts standing in AdjN and VN dependency relations. The approach proposed by Turney et al. (2011) derives concreteness information using a small seed set of concrete and abstract terms and a corpus-based method for inferring the values for the remaining words. This information was used to build a feature for detection of metaphorical AdjN phrases; the methodology was extended in Assaf et al. (2013) and again in Neuman et al. (2013) to provide more sophisticated methods of measuring concreteness and using this information for classifying AdjN and VN pairs. Gandy et al. (2013) extended Turney et al. (2011) algorithm to be more sensitive to the fact that a certain concrete facet might be more or less salient for the given concept. Tsvetkov et al. (2014) used a supervised learning approach to predict concreteness ratings for terms by extending the MRC concreteness ratings. Hill and Korhonen (2014) used Brysbaert et al. (2013) data to obtain values for the concreteness of nouns, and derived the values for adjectives using average concreteness of nouns occurring with the adjectives in a background corpus. Apart from the exact source of the concreteness values, our work differs from these studies in that we evaluate the impact of the concreteness-related measures on an overall word-level metaphor classification system that attempts to classify every content word in a running text. In contrast, the approaches above were evaluated using data specially constructed to evaluate the algorithms, that is, using isolated AdjN or VN pairs.

The problem of machine learning with class-imbalanced datasets has been extensively researched; see He and Garcia (2009) for a review. Yang et al. (2014) and Muller et al. (2014) specifically evaluated the AutoWeighting technique on two different linguistic classfication tasks against a resamping-based technique, and found the former to yield better performance.

11 Conclusion

In this paper, we presented a supervised machine learning system for word-level classification of all content words in a running text as being metaphorical or non-metaphorical. The system provides a substantial improvement upon a previously published baseline, using re-weighting of the training examples and using features derived from a concreteness database. We observe that while the first manipulation was very effective, the second was only slightly so. Possible reasons for these observations are discussed.

Data	UPT			UPT+ CUpDown+ DCUpDown		
	P	R	F	P	R	F
A-B	.714	.337	.458	.712	.362	.480
B-A	.573	.480	.522	.565	.494	.527
Set A	.693	.462	.552	.699	.475	.564
Set B	.767	.576	.657	.760	.604	.672
Av.	.687	.464	.547	.684	.484	.561
Acad.	.635	.347	.418	.636	.356	.425
Conv.	.506	.240	.316	.487	.236	.309
Fiction	.549	.288	.374	.559	.309	.395
News	.641	.457	.531	.636	.466	.536
Av.	.583	.333	.410	.580	.342	.416

A-B	.513	.693	.590	.528	.713	.607
B-A	.400	.647	.494	.415	.670	.513
Set A	.498	.741	.594	.500	.747	.597
Set B	.568	.775	.655	.592	.773	.669
Av.	.495	.714	.583	.509	.726	.597
Acad.	.524	.651	.558	.525	.657	.562
Conv.	.292	.688	.392	.293	.691	.396
Fiction	.400	.600	.476	.411	.607	.486
News	.529	.665	.587	.530	.673	.590
Av.	.436	.651	.503	.440	.657	.509

A-B	.578	.597	.587	.593	.556	.574
B-A	.502	.612	.552	.485	.635	.550
Set A	.558	.659	.602	.561	.661	.604
Set B	.645	.705	.671	.662	.722	.690
Av.	.571	.643	.603	.575	.644	.605
Acad.	.521	.671	.565	.531	.655	.564
Conv.	.321	.614	.404	.293	.691	.396
Fiction	.398	.620	.481	.414	.621	.493
News	.506	.711	.586	.513	.709	.590
Av.	.437	.654	.509	.438	.669	.511

Table 9: Performance of a model without any concreteness features (UPT) and the model UPT+CUpDown+DCUpDown, in no-reweighting regime (top), auto-weighting (middle), and optimal weighting (bottom).

References

Dan Assaf, Yair Neuman, Yohai Cohen, Shlomo Argamon, Newton Howard, Mark Last, Ophir Frieder, and Moshe Koppel. 2013. Why "dark thoughts" aren't really dark: A novel algorithm for metaphor identification. In *Proc. IEEE Symposium Series on Computational Intelligence 2013*, Singapore.

Beata Beigman Klebanov and Michael Flor. 2013. Argumentation-relevant metaphors in test-taker essays. In *Proceedings of the First Workshop on Metaphor in NLP*, pages 11–20, Atlanta, Georgia, June. Association for Computational Linguistics.

Beata Beigman Klebanov, Chee Wee Leong, Michael Heilman, and Michael Flor. 2014. Different texts, same metaphors: Unigrams and beyond. In *Proceedings of the Second Workshop on Metaphor in NLP*, pages 11–17, Baltimore, MD, June. Association for Computational Linguistics.

Steven Bethard, Vicky Tzuyin Lai, and James Martin. 2009. Topic model analysis of metaphor frequency for psycholinguistic stimuli. In *Proceedings of the Workshop on Computational Approaches to Linguistic Creativity*, CALC '09, pages 9–16, Stroudsburg, PA, USA. Association for Computational Linguistics.

Daniel Blanchard, Michael Heilman, and Nitin Madnani. 2013. SciKit-Learn Laboratory. GitHub repository, https://github.com/EducationalTestingService/skll.

David M. Blei, Andrew Y. Ng, and Michael I. Jordan. 2003. Latent Dirichlet Allocation. *Journal of Machine Learning Research*, 3:993–1022.

Marc Brysbaert, Amy Beth Warriner, and Victor Kuperman. 2013. Concreteness ratings for 40 thousand generally known english word lemmas. *Behavior Research Methods*, pages 1–8.

Marie-Catherine de Marneffe, Bill MacCartney, and Christopher Manning. 2006. Generating Typed Dependency Parses from Phrase Structure Parses. In *Proceedings of LREC*, pages 449–454, Genoa, Italy, May.

Jonathan Dunn. 2013. What metaphor identification systems can tell us about metaphor-in-language. In *Proceedings of the First Workshop on Metaphor in NLP*, pages 1–10, Atlanta, Georgia, June. Association for Computational Linguistics.

Jonathan Dunn. 2014. Multi-dimensional abstractness in cross-domain mappings. In *Proceedings of the Second Workshop on Metaphor in NLP*, pages 27–32, Baltimore, MD, June. Association for Computational Linguistics.

Lisa Gandy, Nadji Allan, Mark Atallah, Ophir Frieder, Newton Howard, Sergey Kanareykin, Moshe Koppel, Mark Last, Yair Neuman, and Shlomo Argamon. 2013. Automatic identification of conceptual metaphors with limited knowledge.

Haibo He and Edwardo Garcia. 2009. Learning from imbalanced data. *IEEE Transactions on Knowledge and Data Engineering*, 21(9):12631284.

Felix Hill and Anna Korhonen. 2014. Concreteness and subjectivity as dimensions of lexical meaning. In *Proceedings of the 52nd Annual Meeting of the Association for Computational Linguistics, ACL 2014, June 22-27, 2014, Baltimore, MD, USA, Volume 2: Short Papers*, pages 725–731.

Dirk Hovy, Shashank Shrivastava, Sujay Kumar Jauhar, Mrinmaya Sachan, Kartik Goyal, Huying Li, Whitney Sanders, and Eduard Hovy. 2013. Identifying metaphorical word use with tree kernels. In *Proceedings of the First Workshop on Metaphor in NLP*, pages 52–57, Atlanta, Georgia, June. Association for Computational Linguistics.

Hyeju Jang, Mario Piergallini, Miaomiao Wen, and Carolyn Rose. 2014. Conversational metaphors in use: Exploring the contrast between technical and everyday notions of metaphor. In *Proceedings of the Second Workshop on Metaphor in NLP*, pages 1–10, Baltimore, MD, June. Association for Computational Linguistics.

Michael Mohler, David Bracewell, Marc Tomlinson, and David Hinote. 2013. Semantic signatures for example-based linguistic metaphor detection. In *Proceedings of the First Workshop on Metaphor in NLP*, pages 27–35, Atlanta, Georgia, June. Association for Computational Linguistics.

Philippe Muller, Cécile Fabre, and Clémentine Adam. 2014. Predicting the relevance of distributional semantic similarity with contextual information. In *Proceedings of the 52nd Annual Meeting of the Association for Computational Linguistics (Volume 1: Long Papers)*, pages 479–488, Baltimore, Maryland, June. Association for Computational Linguistics.

Yair Neuman, Dan Assaf, Yohai Cohen, Mark Last, Shlomo Argamon, Newton Howard, and Ophir Frieder. 2013. Metaphor identification in large texts corpora. *PLoS ONE*, 8(4), 04.

Bradley Pasanek and D. Sculley. 2008. Mining millions of metaphors. *Literary and Linguistic Computing*, 23(3):345–360.

F. Pedregosa, G. Varoquaux, A. Gramfort, V. Michel, B. Thirion, O. Grisel, M. Blondel, P. Prettenhofer, R. Weiss, V. Dubourg, J. Vanderplas, A. Passos, D. Cournapeau, M. Brucher, M. Perrot, and E. Duchesnay. 2011. Scikit-learn: Machine Learning in Python. *Journal of Machine Learning Research*, 12:2825–2830.

Evan Sandhaus. 2008. The New York Times Annotated Corpus. LDC Catalog No: LDC2008T19.

Marc Schulder and Eduard Hovy. 2014. Metaphor detection through term relevance. In *Proceedings of the Second Workshop on Metaphor in NLP*, pages 18–26, Baltimore, MD, June. Association for Computational Linguistics.

Ekaterina Shutova and Lin Sun. 2013. Unsupervised metaphor identification using hierarchical graph factorization clustering. In *Proceedings of HLT-NAACL*, pages 978–988.

Ekaterina Shutova, Simone Teufel, and Anna Korhonen. 2013. Statistical metaphor processing. *Computational Linguistics*, 39(1).

Gerard Steen, Aletta Dorst, Berenike Herrmann, Anna Kaal, Tina Krennmayr, and Trijntje Pasma. 2010. *A Method for Linguistic Metaphor Identification*. Amsterdam: John Benjamins.

Tomek Strzalkowski, George Aaron Broadwell, Sarah Taylor, Laurie Feldman, Samira Shaikh, Ting Liu, Boris Yamrom, Kit Cho, Umit Boz, Ignacio Cases, and Kyle Elliot. 2013. Robust extraction of metaphor from novel data. In *Proceedings of the First Workshop on Metaphor in NLP*, pages 67–76, Atlanta, Georgia, June. Association for Computational Linguistics.

Kristina Toutanova, Dan Klein, Christopher D. Manning, and Yoram Singer. 2003. Feature-rich part-of-speech tagging with a cyclic dependency network. In *Proceedings of the 2003 Conference of the North American Chapter of the Association for Computational Linguistics on Human Language Technology - Volume 1*, NAACL '03, pages 173–180, Stroudsburg, PA, USA. Association for Computational Linguistics.

Yulia Tsvetkov, Elena Mukomel, and Anatole Gershman. 2013. Cross-lingual metaphor detection using common semantic features. In *Proceedings of the First Workshop on Metaphor in NLP*, pages 45–51, Atlanta, Georgia, June. Association for Computational Linguistics.

Yulia Tsvetkov, Leonid Boytsov, Anatole Gershman, Eric Nyberg, and Chris Dyer. 2014. Metaphor detection with cross-lingual model transfer. In *Proceedings of the 52nd Annual Meeting of the Association for Computational Linguistics (Volume 1: Long Papers)*, pages 248–258, Baltimore, Maryland, June. Association for Computational Linguistics.

Peter Turney, Yair Neuman, Dan Assaf, and Yohai Cohen. 2011. Literal and metaphorical sense identification through concrete and abstract context. In *Proceedings of the Conference on Empirical Methods in Natural Language Processing*, pages 680–690, Stroudsburg, PA, USA. Association for Computational Linguistics.

Xuesong Yang, Anastassia Loukina, and Keelan Evanini. 2014. Machine learning approaches to improving pronunciation error detection on an imbalanced corpus. In *Proceedings of IEEE 2014 Spoken Language Technology Workshop, South Lake Tahoe, USA*, pages 300–305.

Modeling the interaction between sensory and affective meanings for detecting metaphor

Andrew Gargett
School of Computer Science
University of Birmingham
United Kingdom
A.D.Gargett@cs.bham.ac.uk

John Barnden
School of Computer Science
University of Birmingham
United Kingdom
J.A.Barnden@cs.bham.ac.uk

Abstract

Concreteness and imageability have long been held to play an important role in the meanings of figurative expressions. Recent work has implemented this idea in order to detect metaphors in natural language discourse. Yet, a relatively unexplored dimension of metaphor is the role of affective meanings. In this paper, we will show how combining concreteness, imageability and sentiment scores, as features at different linguistic levels, improves performance in such tasks as automatic detection of metaphor in discourse. By gradually refining these features through descriptive studies, we found the best performing classifier for our task to be random forests. Further refining of our classifiers for part-of-speech, led to very promising results, with $F1$ scores of .744 for nouns,.799 for verbs, .811 for prepositions. We suggest that our approach works by capturing to some degree the complex interactions between external sensory information (concreteness), information about internal experience (imageability), and relatively subjective meanings (sentiment), in the use of metaphorical expressions in natural language.

1 Introduction

Figurative language plays an important role in "grounding" our communication in the world around us. Being able to talk about "the journey of life", "getting into a relationship", whether there are "strings attached" to a contract, or even just "surfing the internet", are important and useful aspects of everyday meaning-making practices. Much recent work on modeling metaphor, especially using computational techniques, has concentrated on more inter-subjective aspects of such meanings, such as the way that figurative expressions are apparently used to inject meanings that are somehow more "concrete" into daily discourse (Turney et al., 2011; Tsvetkov et al., 2013).On such an account, describing love as a journey, or life as a test, is a way of casting a fairly abstract idea, such as love or life, in more concrete and everyday terms, such as a journey or a test. Related dimensions of figurative meanings, such as imageability, having to do with how readily the concept expressed by some linguistic item brings an image to mind, have also been investigated (Cacciari and Glucksberg, 1995; Gibbs, 2006; Urena and Faber, 2010).

Work across a range of disciplines has begun examining the complex interaction between metaphor and the intra-subjective emotional meanings expressed at all levels of language (Kövecses, 2003; Meier and Robinson, 2005; Strzalkowski et al., 2014), although modelling such interaction has proved to be somewhat challenging. For example, while a native speaker of some language can be expected to consistently and reliably rate isolated words for their levels of valence ("pleasantness"), arousal ("emotional intensity") and dominance ("control") (Warriner et al., 2013), the same cannot be expected for more complex expressions such as "the journey of life" or "strings attached". Whether there are indeed systematic and stable patterns for the intra-subjective meanings of such expressions is still an open question.

Proceedings of the Third Workshop on Metaphor in NLP, pages 21–30,
Denver, Colorado, June 5, 2015.

Linking these two components of figurative meaning, while it has been understood for some time that concreteness and imageability very strongly correlate (Paivio et al., 1968), recent work has suggested strong reasons for rethinking this. On the contrary, (Dellantonio et al., 2014) suggest that concreteness and imageability are in fact quite different psychological constructs, and the basis for this difference is that imageability involves both "external sensory information" as well as "internal bodily-related sensory experience," whereas concreteness ratings capture only external sensory information. From this apparent difference internal vs. external sensory information, they derive an index of the "weight" such internal sensory information has in relation to individual word meaning, which can be derived as the difference between the concreteness and imageability of a word. Labelling this weight as **w**, we could symbolise this idea as follows:

$$\mathbf{w} = |(\text{CONC - IMAG})|$$

This will allow us to more clearly separate concreteness from imageability in our modelling, and so better examine the interactions of each with sentiment in processing metaphor.

There has been much work on the interaction between metaphor and sentiment (Fainsilber and Ortony, 1987; Fussell and Moss, 1998; Littlemore and Low, 2006). Metaphor researchers have long recognised that metaphor and affective communication are central to each other: metaphor is a central way of conveying affect, and conversely conveying affect is a central function of metaphor. However, it is important to distinguish between (a) using metaphor to describe an emotion (e.g. "anger swept through me") vs. (b) emotion being conveyed through connotations of source terms (e.g. "terrorism is a form of cancer", where negative affect about cancer carries over to terrorism).[1] However, there is still much more work to do in elucidating these complex connections.

Motivated by such considerations, we focus here on how concreteness, imageability, and affective meaning, interact in metaphorical expressions, and to this end we have examined a large corpus annotated for metaphor, the Vrije University Amsterdam Metaphor Corpus (VUAMC) (Steen et al., 2010), with respect to such fetures as imageability and concreteness, as well as valence, arousal and dominance. The background for these studies is our ongoing work on devising a computational tool for detecting, and to some degree, also understanding, metaphor.[2]

2 Method

2.1 Data

Our data comes from the Vrije University Amsterdam Metaphor Corpus (VUAMC), consisting of over 188,000 words selected from the British National Corpus-Baby (BNC-Baby), and annotated for metaphor using the Metaphor Identification Procedure (MIP) (Steen et al., 2010). The MIP involves annotators considering individuals words from the corpus, and answering the question (somewhat simplified here): does this word have a more "basic" meaning[3] than its current "contextual" meaning, with the latter also being understandable in comparison with the former? If the answer is "yes", the current item is used metaphorically, else it is used non-metaphorically.

The corpus itself has four registers, of between 44,000 and 50,000 words each: academic texts, news texts, fiction, and conversations, with over 23,600 words were annotated as metaphorical across the 4 registers.[4] Table (1) lists statistics for the VUAMC from (Steen et al., 2010), specifically presenting standardised residuals (SRs) for counts of metaphorical vs. non-metaphorical nouns, verbs and prepositions lexical units, and of[5] SRs usefully enable pinpointing interesting deviations of the observed frequency for items occurring in specific categories in our sample from the frequency we actually expect for them given their overall frequency

[1] In order to maintain anonymity, references to this latter work are suppressed during the review period.

[2] Reference suppressed during the period of review.

[3] Defined in terms of being *more concrete*, *related to bodily actions*, *more precise*, and *historically older*, see (Steen et al., 2010) for details.

[4] The VUAMC is available from: `http://ota.ahds.ac.uk/desc/2541.html`

[5] More strictly, they refer to so-called *metaphor-related words*, i.e. a word the use of which "may potentially be explained by some form of cross-domain mapping from a more basic meaning of that word."

in the entire sample.[6] For example, while there are far fewer nouns in all registers except Conversations, prepositions occur with far greater than expected frequency in all registers, and verbs are similar to prepositions, although not as extreme, in occurring with greater than expected frequency in all registers. The VUAMC is usefully balanced across 4 registers, making it highly useful for our ongoing work on automatic metaphor annotation.

2.2 Procedure

2.2.1 Pre-processing

We have enriched the VUAMC in several ways. First, we have parsed the corpus using the graph-based version of the Mate tools dependency parser (Bohnet, 2010), adding rich syntactic information.[7] Second, we have incorporated the MRC Psycholinguistic Database (Wilson, 1988), a dictionary of 150,837 words, with different subsets of these words having been rated by human subjects in psycholinguistic experiments.[8] Of special note, the database includes 4,295 words rated with degrees of concreteness, these ratings ranging from 158 (meaning *highly abstract*) to 670 (meaning *highly concrete*), and also 9,240 words rated for degrees of imageability, which is taken to indicate how easily a word can evoke mental imagery, these ratings also ranging between 100 and 700 (a higher score indicating greater imageability). The concreteness scores (and to some extent the imageability ones also) have been used extensively for work on metaphor, e.g. (Turney et al., 2011; Tsvetkov et al., 2013). Finally, we have incorporated the work by (Warriner et al., 2013) on the Affective Norms for English Words (ANEW), which provides 13,915 English content words, rated for: valence (measuring the "pleasantness" of the word), arousal ("emotional intensity" of the word) and dominance (the degree of "control" evoked by the thing that the word denotes). This latter dataset includes rich statistical information (such as means and variance) for these scores, which we make use of in our work.

Combining these resources, we extend the VUAMC with information about dependency relations, concreteness, imageability, valence, arousal and dominance. However, this combination is not without problems, for example, the VUAMC data set is much larger than the MRC data set, so that many VUAMC words have no MRC scores, and we need a smoothing procedure; a similar disparity in size exists between the VUAMC corpus and the ANEW scores. Now, a key finding in the literature is that POS strongly correlates with metaphor; Table (1) illustrates this quite well, and we have carried out various studies in this direction (see below). As a first approximation, we smooth such discrepancies between the VUAMC and MRC, by calculating an average MRC score for each POS across the entire corpus, as follows: first, from VUAMC words with MRC scores, we calculated an average MRC score (concreteness/imageability) by POS across all the the VUAMC data, second, those VUAMC words without MRC scores (i.e. missing from the MRC database) could then be assigned a score based on their POS. We did the same for the ANEW scores, but this time not in terms of POS, which is missing from ANEW: we maintained average ANEW scores, and gave these to VUAMC items not represented in the ANEW dataset. However, this kind of naive "global" average is not very discriminative of the key difference we are trying to model between metaphorical vs. non-metaphorical expressions, and we are currently re-implementing our smoothing strategy.[9]

2.2.2 Experimental design

We carried out a preliminary study, followed by three main studies, using the pre-processed data described in Section (2.2.1). Below we list the aims, hypotheses and procedures for these studies.

Preliminary study. This initial study aimed to select features for use in subsequent machine learning studies. In particular, we covered features considered important for the task in previous literature. We

[6]For a proper appreciation of the statistics, please see the relevant sections of (Steen et al., 2010).

[7]Note this includes POS tagging, POS tags rich enough to capture such distinctions as common nouns vs. personal nouns, participles vs. independent verbs vs. copula verbs, etc – see: `https://code.google.com/p/mate-tools/`.

[8]`http://ota.oucs.ox.ac.uk/headers/1054.xml`

[9]Thanks to the reviewers for this workshop for noting this issue; although, it we should point out that the planning phase for re-implementing this aspect of our work pre-dates submission of this paper.

POS	Academic		News		Fiction		Conversation	
	Lit.	Met.	Lit.	Met.	Lit.	Met.	Lit.	Met.
Nouns	82.4 (1.2)	17.6 (-2.5)	86.8 (4.0)	13.2 (-9.1)	89.5 (1.4)	10.5 (-3.8)	91.7 (-0.4)	8.3 (1.5)
Prepositions	57.5 (-21.4)	42.5 (45.0)	61.9 (-17.0)	38.1 (38.5)	66.6 (-14.9)	33.4 (40.6)	66.2 (-13.5)	33.8 (46.9)
Verbs	72.3 (-9.2)	27.7 (19.3)	72.4 (-10.9)	27.6 (24.6)	84.1 (-4.2)	15.9 (11.6)	90.9 (-1.7)	9.1 (5.7)

Table 1: Percentages of POS and metaphors per register, with standardised residuals in brackets (n=47934)

were seeking to discover the optimal combination of features for discriminating between literal and non-literal words.

Study 1. This study aimed to find a suitable learning algorithm, for predicting literal vs. nonliteral expressions. In addition, we also examined the relative importance of particular independent variables, for predicting literal vs. nonliteral expressions, by sampling a range of standard machine learning algorithms,[10] and from this we arrived at a smaller set of more viable learning algorithms, specifically, random forests (**rf**), gradient boosting machines (**gbm**), k nearest neighbours (**knn**), and support vector machines (**svm**). In addition, we considered different combinations of the features collected in the preliminary studies. The resulting models (learning algorithms, plus combinations of features) were chosen because they showed promising performance, and adequately represented the range of models used for similar tasks in other studies elsewhere. This study coincided with the initial phase in developing our system for automatically annotating metaphor, and for this early development version of our system, we constructed a random sample covering 80% of the VUAMC.

For evaluation, we compared results for each target model against a baseline model, this latter being the best single variable model we found in earlier studies, which can predict whether a word is metaphorical or not, based simply on the concreteness score for that word. Results consisted of comparing confusion matrices for ground truth vs. the output of each model, trained on a training set of 60% of the data, then these models were tuned with a testing set of 20% of the data. Finally using a validation set of the remaining 20% of the data, accuracy, precision, recall and F1 scores were calculated for each model.

Study 2. For this next study, focusing on the Random Forests algorithm, we extended our preliminary studies in a quite natural way, and separated the classifiers according to POS, separately training random forest classifiers on our original data set split into nouns, verbs and prepositions. The training setup used here was largely the same as the one used for Study 1, except that the entire VUAMC data set was employed for this study.

Study 3. Finally, having identified various dimensions of metaphorical meaning, and having set out to validate the interaction between these dimensions in Studies 1 and 2, we next turned to possible explanations of the patterns we observed across, for example, different POS. Starting from the random forest classifiers we had trained on the VUAMC in study 2, it was apparent that the sheer number of trees used by such classifiers means they are far from being readily interpretable; nevertheless, we explored the use of recent tools for attempting to improve the interpretability of these kinds of ensemble classifiers.[11]

[10]Specifically, we considered linear discriminant analysis, k nearest neighbours, naive bayes, random forest, gradient boosting machines, logistic regression, support vector machines.

[11]In particular, we employed the "inTrees" R package for this (Deng, 2014) – see also: `http://cran.r-project.org/web/packages/inTrees/index.html`.

3 Results

3.1 Preliminary study

In earlier work (Gargett et al., 2014), we examined the role of concreteness and imageability in capturing the variation between nonliteral vs. literal expressions, for heads vs. their dependents. Figures (1) and (2) suggest that making this kind of fine-grained distinction within our data set between heads and their dependents, enables capturing variation between literal and nonliteral items for some POS; for example, nonliteral head nouns appear to have higher MRC scores than their dependents, distinct from literal head nouns (verbs appear to make no such distinction). While literal and nonliteral head prepositions both seem indistinguishable from their dependents in terms of concreteness scores, nonliteral head prepositions seem to have imageability scores quite distinct from their dependents.

As can be seen from Figures (1) and (2), our initial study failed to capture variation between verbs. As a follow-up, we incorporated features from the ANEW data set; initial results are plotted in Figure (3), and the variation exibited across all POS in this plot suggest, e.g., a possible role for arousal in distinguishing literal from nonliteral verbs.

3.2 Study 1

Next, we focused on selecting a learning algorithm, for predicting literal vs. nonliteral expressions. The features used here are drawn from our earlier studies, directly incorporating the various scores from the MRC and ANEW databases. Results are displayed in Table (2), with the boxed cell in this table showing the strongest performing combination of learning model and features, which turned out to be all features from the MRC and ANEW scores, trained using random forests.

3.3 Study 2

In Table (3), we present the results for our study of different random forest models by POS. The metrics we used here are standard: harmonic mean of recall and precision, or **F1**, and the overall agreement rate between model and validation set, or **accuracy**. A clear effect when including the "weight" term w can be seen (recall this was the difference between concreteness and imageability). The clear winners in each vertical comparison (e.g. between F1 for **Verbs** vs. **Verbs**$_w$) is shown in this table. We will come back to a discussion of the significance of these results in Section (4) below.

3.4 Study 3

Our next study sets out to try to interpret in some way the results from Study 2, and Tables (4) to (6) present the rule conditions extracted from a sample of the first 100 trees for each random forest model for each POS. Important measures of the performance of the classifiers given here include **err**, the so-called out-of-bag (OOB) error estimate, and **freq**, the proportion of occurrences of instances of this rule. OOB error rate is a statistic calculated internally while running the algorithm, and has been shown to be unbiased: while constructing trees, a bootstrap sample is taken from the original data, with some proportion (e.g. about a third) left out, which can be used as a test set while a particular tree is being built, and in this way, a test classification can be obtained for each case in this same proportion (say, about a third) of trees. The error rate is then the proportion of times this test classification was wrong.

Ensemble methods such as random forests are notoriously opaque, largely due to the sheer volume of trees constructed during model building, thereby making clear interpretation of these models problematic (Breiman, 2002; Zhang and Wang, 2009); and yet, they have also emerged as one of the best performing learning models,[12] and work very well for classification tasks such as ours. Consequently, there is broad interest in better interpretation of such models, and development in this direction is ongoing.

Many of the trees built by such ensemble methods,[13] typically contain not only trees crucial for classification performance, but also many which could be removed without significant impact on performance. Proceeding along these lines, "pruning" the forest can result in a smaller, and thus more interpretable, set of trees, without significant impact on performance; from this smaller set, it is more feasi-

[12] As witnessed in several recent Kaggle competitions, `https://www.kaggle.com/wiki/RandomForests`.

[13] Other relevant methods we are currently investigating include gradient boosting machines.

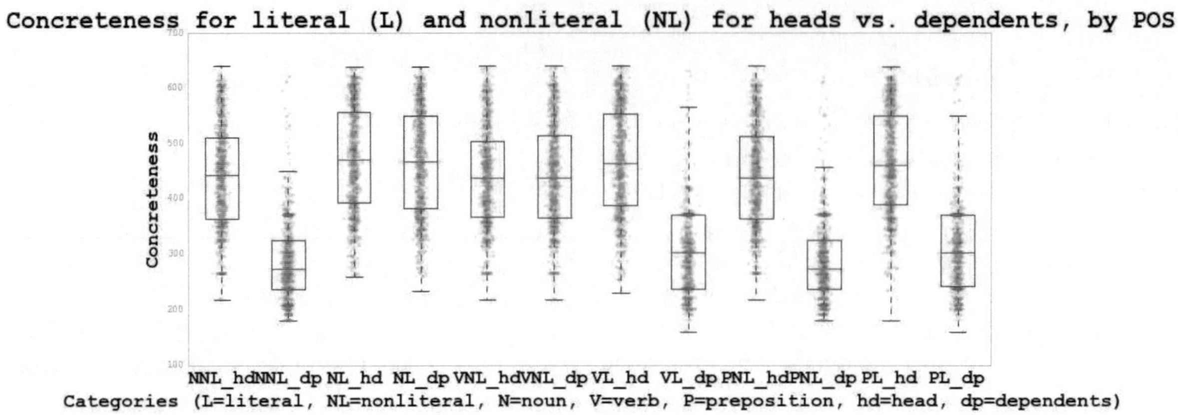

Figure 1: Plot of concreteness scores for literal vs. nonliteral/metaphorical heads vs. their dependents, in the VUAMC, grouped by parts of speech

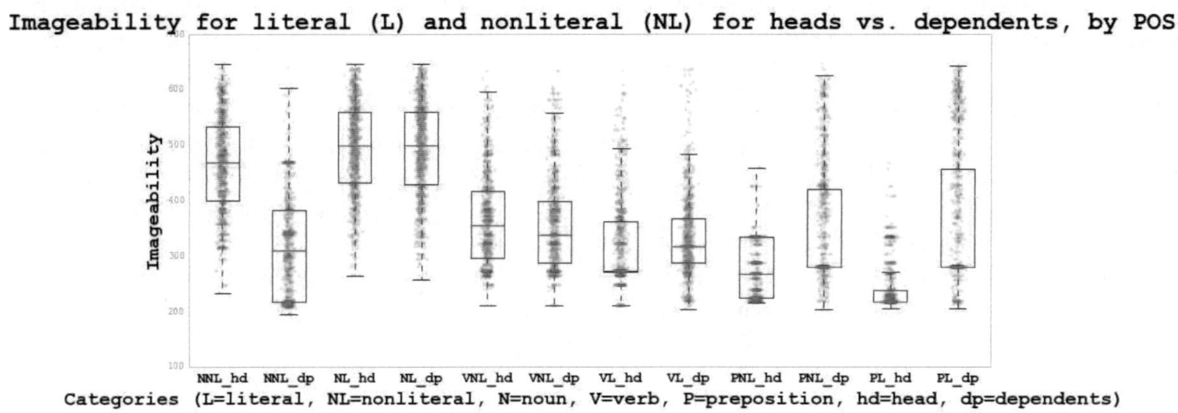

Figure 2: Plot of imageability scores for literal vs. nonliteral/metaphorical heads vs. their dependents, in the VUAMC, grouped by parts of speech

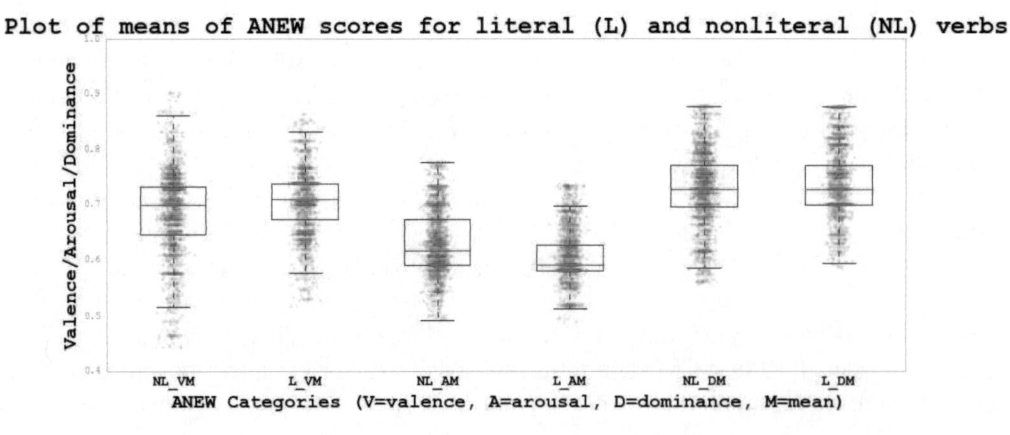

Figure 3: Plot of anew scores for literal vs. nonliteral/metaphorical verbs in the VUAMC

ble that a relatively transparent set of rules for constructing some significant proportion of trees could

Models	**Full**	**Minimal**	**MRC**	**ANEW**	**Base**
gbm	0.7542	0.7364	0.7266	0.7051	0.6673
knn	0.6945	0.6793	0.6861	0.6823	0.6802
rf	0.7813	0.7362	0.7275	0.7144	0.6906
svm	0.6787	0.6689	0.6396	0.6690	0.6348

Table 2: Results (F1) of evaluating models with different combinations of features, for predicting non/literal items (n=3574)

POS	**Accuracy**	**F1**	**n**
Nouns	0.733	0.737	1470
Nouns$_w$	0.743	0.744	1470
Verbs	0.7870	0.799	2216
Verbs$_w$	0.7866	0.798	2216
Prepositions	0.785	0.801	2294
Prepositions$_w$	0.790	0.811	2295

Table 3: Results (Accuracy, F1) for random forest models for different POS, for predicting non/literal items, for models with and without the "weight" term **w**

len	**freq**	**err**	**condition**	**prediction**
1	0.059	0.019	**pos** $\leq$ 1.037	L
1	0.213	0.367	**imag** $>$ 0.544	L
3	0.071	0.194	**VSDSum** $\leq$ -0.469 **&** **ASDSum** $\leq$ -0.891 **&** **DRatSum** $\leq$ -0.1925	NL
3	0.225	0.396	**AMeanSum** $\leq$ -0.597 **&** **DMeanSum** $>$ -0.272 **&** **w** $\leq$ 0.121	L
2	0.012	0.477	**conc** $>$ 1.030 **&** **DMeanSum** $\leq$ -0.480	NL

Table 4: Rules extracted from random forest models for Nouns (len=length of condition, freq=proportion of data instances meeting condition, err=proportion of incorrectly classified instances as over instances meeting condition, SD=standard deviation)

be extracted – this smaller set of rules could in principle be used to attempt an interpretation of the resulting model.

The results presented here are illustrative only, being based on a sample of the first 100 trees from each classifier built for each POS. Looking across these tables, we see some evidence of commonality for some features across different POS; for example, extensive use of the "weight" term **w** is made across POS (see Section (1) about this).[14] On the other hand, there are also quite distinct combinations of

[14]Note also the use of the feature **pos**, which utilises the finer POS distinctions made by the Mate tools (see Section (2.2.1) about this).

len	freq	err	condition	prediction
2	0.442	0.316	**imag** > -1.945 **&** **depslist_DSDSum_mean** > -3.530	NL
2	0.102	0.21	**imag** ≤ -1.578 **&** **w** ≤ -0.013	L
2	0.073	0.192	**DMeanSum** > 1.146 **&** **depslist_DSDSum_mean** ≤ -3.530	L
1	0.116	0.414	**DMeanSum** > 1.274	L
2	0.218	0.4	**ARatSum** ≤ -0.019 **&** **DRatSum** > -0.222	NL
2	0.534	0.395	**imag** > -1.827 **&** **depslist_imag_mean** > -0.990	NL

Table 5: Rules extracted from random forest models for Verbs (len=length of condition, freq=proportion of data instances meeting condition, err=proportion of incorrectly classified instances for instances meeting condition, SD=standard deviation, depslist=list of dependents)

len	freq	err	condition	prediction
1	0.73	0.349	**imag** > -1.124	NL
2	0.413	0.313	**w** > -0.0881 **&** **w** ≤ 0.518	NL
2	0.039	0.217	**w** ≤ 0.110 **&** **w** > 0.066	L
1	0.53	0.336	**imag** > -1.023	NL

Table 6: Rules extracted from random forest models for Prepositions (len=length of condition, freq=proportion of data instances meeting condition, err=proportion of incorrectly classified instances for instances meeting condition)

concreteness, imageability, **w**, and a small but interesting subset of the ANEW categories, across POS. For example, while nouns make good use of concreteness, imageability and **w**, combinations of imageability and **w** are prevalent for verbs and prepositions. Further, nouns and verbs, being content words, seem to make good use of the ANEW features, but prepositions make no use of such features, perhaps due to their status as function words. More careful study of a wider range of rules, as well as possible conditioning environments is required, and such suggestions remain tentative. Note also that one complication in all of this is that there are extensive errors for most of the extracted rules, and close study of possible sources of such errors is planned for future work.

4 Discussion

In this paper, we presented results from various studies we conducted to help us refine features, and determine suitable training algorithms for our automatic metaphor detection system. The training regime included training separate classifiers for distinct POS (nouns, verbs, prepositions), and also implements suggestions from psycholinguistics, (Dellantonio et al., 2014), to model the interaction between concreteness, imageability and sentiment as dimensions of figurative meaning, in particular, distinguishing concreteness from imageability as the feature **w** (i.e. the difference between concreteness and imageability scores for individual lexical items). Incorporating **w** led to marked improvement in our classifier performance, and we reported very competitive performance for this system: achieving an **FI** of over .81 for prepositions, and just below .80 for verbs, with nouns achieving just under .75. Finally, we have attempted to go beyond detection, toward trying to interpret the models we are using, which has led to a tentative proposal regarding function vs. content words in our approach, in terms of the features being used for classification: whereas content words such as nouns and verbs use the full range of the MRC and ANEW scores, function words like prepositions tend to use a much sparer combinations of features, such as the derived score **w** together with imageability. We are currently trying to exploit these and other insights to further improve system performance.

Acknowledgments

Thanks go to the organisers of the workshop; as well as to the anonymous reviewers who provided very helpful feedback, although, of course, we alone remain responsible for the final version. We acknowledge financial support through a Marie Curie International Incoming Fellowship (project 330569) awarded to both authors (A.G. as fellow, J.B. as P.I.).

References

Bernd Bohnet. 2010. Very high accuracy and fast dependency parsing is not a contradiction. In *The 23rd International Conference on Computational Linguistics (COLING 2010), Beijing, China.*

Leo Breiman. 2002. Looking inside the black box. Technical report, Department of Statistics, California University. Wald Lecture II.

Christina Cacciari and Sam Glucksberg. 1995. Imaging idiomatic expressions: literal or figurative meanings. *Idioms: Structural and psychological perspectives*, pages 43–56.

Sara Dellantonio, Claudio Mulatti, Luigi Pastore, and Remo Job. 2014. Measuring inconsistencies can lead you forward. the case of imageability and concreteness ratings. *Language Sciences*, 5:708.

Houtao Deng. 2014. Interpreting tree ensembles with intrees. Technical report, Intuit. arXiv:1408.5456.

Lynn Fainsilber and Andrew Ortony. 1987. Metaphorical uses of language in the expression of emotions. *Metaphor and Symbol*, 2(4):239–250.

Susan R Fussell and Mallie M Moss. 1998. Figurative language in emotional communication. *Social and cognitive approaches to interpersonal communication*, pages 113–141.

Andrew Gargett, Josef Ruppenhofer, and John Barnden. 2014. Dimensions of metaphorical meaning. In Michael Zock, Reinhard Rapp, and Chu-Ren Huang, editors, *Proceedings of the 4th Workshop on Cognitive Aspects of the Lexicon (COGALEX)*, pages 166–173.

Raymond W Gibbs. 2006. Metaphor interpretation as embodied simulation. *Mind & Language*, 21(3):434–458.

Zoltán Kövecses. 2003. *Metaphor and emotion: Language, culture, and body in human feeling*. Cambridge University Press.

Jeannette Littlemore and Graham Low. 2006. *Figurative thinking and foreign language learning*. Palgrave Macmillan Houndmills/New York.

Brian P Meier and Michael D Robinson. 2005. The metaphorical representation of affect. *Metaphor and Symbol*, 20(4):239–257.

Allan Paivio, John C Yuille, and Stephen A Madigan. 1968. Concreteness, imagery, and meaningfulness values for 925 nouns. *Journal of experimental psychology*, 76(1, pt.2):1–25.

G.J. Steen, A.G. Dorst, J.B. Herrmann, A.A. Kaal, and T. Krennmayr. 2010. *A Method for Linguistic Metaphor Identification: From MIP to MIPVU*. Convering Evidence in Language and Communication Research. John Benjamins Publishing Company.

Tomek Strzalkowski, Samira Shaikh, Kit Cho, George Aaron Broadwell, Laurie Feldman, Sarah Taylor, Boris Yamrom, Ting Liu, Ignacio Cases, Yuliya Peshkova, et al. 2014. Computing affect in metaphors. *ACL 2014*, page 42.

Yulia Tsvetkov, Elena Mukomel, and Anatole Gershman. 2013. Cross-lingual metaphor detection using common semantic features. In *Proceedings of the First Workshop on Metaphor in NLP*, pages 45–51, Atlanta, Georgia, June. Association for Computational Linguistics.

Peter D Turney, Yair Neuman, Dan Assaf, and Yohai Cohen. 2011. Literal and metaphorical sense identification through concrete and abstract context. In *Proceedings of the 2011 Conference on the Empirical Methods in Natural Language Processing*, pages 680–690.

Jose Manuel Urena and Pamela Faber. 2010. Reviewing imagery in resemblance and non-resemblance metaphors. *Cognitive Linguistics*, 21(1):123–149.

Amy Beth Warriner, Victor Kuperman, and Marc Brysbaert. 2013. Norms of valence, arousal, and dominance for 13,915 english lemmas. *Behavior research methods*, 45(4):1191–1207.

Michael Wilson. 1988. Mrc psycholinguistic database: Machine-usable dictionary, version 2.00. *Behavior Research Methods, Instruments, & Computers*, 20(1):6–10.

Heping Zhang and Minghui Wang. 2009. Search for the smallest random forest. *Statistics and its Interface*, 2(3):381.

Exploring Sensorial Features for Metaphor Identification

Serra Sinem Tekiroğlu
University of Trento
Fondazione Bruno Kessler
Trento, Italy
tekiroglu@fbk.eu

Gözde Özbal
Fondazione Bruno Kessler
Trento, Italy
gozbalde@gmail.com

Carlo Strapparava
Fondazione Bruno Kessler
Trento, Italy
strappa@fbk.eu

Abstract

Language is the main communication device to represent the environment and share a common understanding of the world that we perceive through our sensory organs. Therefore, each language might contain a great amount of sensorial elements to express the perceptions both in literal and figurative usage. To tackle the semantics of figurative language, several conceptual properties such as concreteness or imegeability are utilized. However, there is no attempt in the literature to analyze and benefit from the sensorial elements for figurative language processing. In this paper, we investigate the impact of sensorial features on metaphor identification. We utilize an existing lexicon associating English words to sensorial modalities and propose a novel technique to automatically discover these associations from a dependency-parsed corpus. In our experiments, we measure the contribution of the sensorial features to the metaphor identification task with respect to a state of the art model. The results demonstrate that sensorial features yield better performance and show good generalization properties.

1 Introduction

Languages include many lexical items that are connected to sensory modalities in various semantic roles. For instance, while some words can be used to describe a perception activity (e.g., *to sniff, to watch, to feel*), others can simply be physical phenomena that can be perceived by sensory receptors (e.g., *light*, *song*, *salt*, *smoke*). Common usage of language, either figurative or literal, can be very dense in terms of sensorial words. As an example, the sentence "*I heard a harmonic melody.*" contains three sensorial words: *to hear* as a perception activity, *harmonic* as a perceived sensorial feature and *melody* as a perceivable phenomenon. The connection to the sense modalities of the words might not be mutually exclusive, that is to say a word can be associated with more than one sense. For instance, the adjective *sweet* could be associated with both *taste* and *smell.*

The description of one kind of sense impression by using words that normally describe another is commonly referred to as *linguistic synaesthesia*[1]. As an example, we can consider the slogans "*The taste of a paradise*" where the sense of sight is combined with the sense of taste or "*Hear the big picture*" where *sight* and *hearing* are merged. Synaesthesia strengthens creative thinking and it is commonly exploited as an imagination boosting tool in advertisement slogans (Pricken, 2008).

Synaesthesia is also commonly used in metaphors. Synaesthesic metaphors use words from one type of sensory modality, such as *sight*, *hearing*, *smell*, *taste* and *touch*, to describe a concept from another modality. In conceptual metaphor theory, metaphor is defined as a systematic mapping between two domains; namely target (or tenor) and source (or vehicle) domains (Lakoff and Johnson, 1980). Such mappings are asymmetric and might not correlate all features from the source domain to the target domain. Systematic studies on synaesthetic metaphors propose that there is a

[1] http://ahdictionary.com/

Proceedings of the Third Workshop on Metaphor in NLP, pages 31–39,
Denver, Colorado, June 5, 2015.

certain directionality of sense modality mappings. (Ullman, 1957), in a very early study, presented this directionality as a linear hierarchy of lower and higher sense modalities. In this hieararchy, modalities are ordered from lower to higher as touch, taste, smell, sound and color. Ullman (1957) proposes that lower modalities tend to occur as the source domain, while higher modalities tend to occur as the target domain. For instance, in the synaesthetic metaphor "*soft light*", the target domain of *seeing* is associated with the source domain of *touching*, while the target domain of *hearing* is associated with the source domain of *tasting* in "*sweet music*". However, later studies (Williams, 1976; Shen, 1997) propose that the mapping in the synaesthetic metaphorical transfer is more complex among the sensory modalities. Williams (1976) constitutes a generalized mapping for the synaesthetic metaphorical transfer by means of the diachronic semantic change of sensorial adjectives. Having regard to the citation dates of adjective meanings from Oxford English Dictionary[2] and Middle English Dictionary[3], the regular transfer rules among the sensorial modalities are introduced.

Several techniques for metaphor identification have been explored, including selectional preference violations (Fass, 1991; Neuman et al., 2013) or verb and noun clustering (Shutova et al., 2010; Birke and Sarkar, 2006; Shutova and Sun, 2013), supervised classification (Gedigian et al., 2006; Mohler et al., 2013; Tsvetkov et al., 2014a). As well as the identification techniques, different cognitive properties such as imageability (Broadwell et al., 2013; Tsvetkov et al., 2014a) and concreteness of the metaphor constituents (Neuman et al., 2013; Turney et al., 2011; Tsvetkov et al., 2014a), or lexical semantic properties such as supersenses (Hovy et al., 2013; Tsvetkov et al., 2014a) have been exploited.

While detecting and interpreting metaphors, imageability and concreteness features are generally utilized to identify the metaphorical transfer from a more concrete to a less concrete or from a more imageable to a less imageable word. However, in synaesthetic metaphors, the imageability or concreteness levels of both tenor and vehicle (or target and source) words can be similar. For instance, according to the MRC Psycholinguistic Database (MRCPD) (Coltheart, 1981) the concreteness (C) and imageability (I) values for target *smell* and source *cold* in the sentence "*The statue has a cold smell.*" are *C:450, I:477* and *C:457, I:531* respectively. Likewise, in the noun phrase "*Sweet silence*" the values are very close to each other (*C:352, I:470* for *silence* and *C:463, I:493* for *sweet*). As demonstrated by these examples, while both imageability and concreteness are related to human senses, these features alone might not be sufficient to model synaesthetic metaphors.

In this paper, we fill in this gap by measuring the contribution of the sensorial features to the identification of metaphors in the form of adjective-noun pairs. We explicitly integrate features that represent the sensorial associations of words for metaphor identification. To achieve that, we both utilize an existing sensorial lexicon and propose to discover these associations from a dependency-parsed corpus. In addition, we exploit the synaesthetic directionality rules proposed by Williams (1976) to encode a degree to which an adjective-noun pair is consistent with the synaesthetic metaphorical transfer. Our experiments show that sensorial associations of words could be useful for the identification of metaphorical expressions.

The rest of the paper is organized as follows. We first review the relevant literature to this study in Section 2. Then in Section 3, we describe the word-sense association resources. In Section 4, we describe the features that we introduce and detail the experiments that we conducted. Finally, in Section 5, we draw our conclusions and outline possible future directions.

2 Related Work

Mohler et al. (2013) exploit a supervised classification approach to detect linguistic metaphors. In this work, they first produce a domain-specific semantic signature which can be found to be encoded in the semantic network (linked senses) of WordNet, Wikipedia[4] links and corpus collocation statistics. A set of binary classifiers are actuated to detect metaphoricity within a text by comparing its seman-

[2]http://www.oed.com/

[3]http://quod.lib.umich.edu/m/med/

[4]http://www.wikipedia.org/

tic signature to the semantic signatures of a set of known metaphors.

Schulder and Hovy (2014) consider the term relevance as an indicator of being non-literal and propose that novel metaphorical words are less prone to occur in the typical vocabulary of a text. The performance of this approach is evaluated both as a standalone metaphor classifier and as a component of a classifier using lexical properties of the words such as part-of-speech roles. The authors state that term relevance could improve the random baselines for both tasks and it could especially be useful in case of a sparse dataset.

Rather than an anomaly in the language or a simple word sense disambiguation problem, a cognitive linguistic view considers metaphor as a method for transferring knowledge from a concrete domain to a more abstract domain (Lakoff and Johnson, 1980). Following this view, Turney et al. (2011) propose an algorithm to classify adjectives and verbs as metaphorical or literal based on their abstractness/concreteness levels in association with the nouns they collocate with. The authors describe words as concrete if they are things, events, and properties that can be perceivable by human senses.

Neuman et al. (2013) extend the abstractness/concreteness model of Turney et al. (2011) with a selectional preference approach in order to detect metaphors consisting of concrete concepts. They focus on three types of metaphors including i) a subject noun and an object noun associated by the verb *to be* (e.g., "God is a king"), ii) the metaphorical verb representing the act of a subject noun on an object noun (e.g., "The war absorbed his energy"), iii) metaphorical adjective-noun phrases (e.g., "sweet kid").

Beigman Klebanov et al. (2014) propose a supervised approach to predict the metaphoricity of all content words with any part-of-speech in a running text. The authors propose a model combining unigram, topic models, POS, and concreteness features. While unigram features contribute the most, concreteness features are found to be effective only for some of the sets.

Based on the hypothesis that on the conceptual level, metaphors are shared across languages, rather than being lexical or language specific, Tsvetkov et al. (2014a) propose a metaphor detection system with cross-lingual model transfer for English that exploits several conceptual semantic features; abstractness and imageability, semantic supersenses, vector space word representations. They focus on two types of metaphors with the subject-verb-object (SVO) and adjective-noun (AN) syntactic relations. As another contribution, they create new metaphor-annotated corpora for English and Russian. In addition, they support the initial hypothesis by showing that the model trained in English can detect metaphors in Spanish, Farsi and Russian by projecting the features from the English model into another language using a bilingual dictionary. To the best of our knowledge, this system is the current state of the art for metaphor detection in English and constitutes the baseline for our experiments.

3 Word-Sense Associations

Following the hypothesis of Broadwell et al. (2013) that "Metaphors are likely to use highly imageable words, and words that are generally more imageable than the surrounding context", we introduce a novel hypothesis that metaphors are likely to also use sensorial words. To extract the sensorial associations of words, we use the following two resources.

3.1 Sensicon

This resource (Tekiroglu et al., 2014) is a large sensorial lexicon that associates 22,684 English words with human senses. It is constructed by employing a two phased computational approach.

In the first phase, a bootstrapping strategy is performed to generate a relatively large set of sensory seed words from a small set of manually selected seed words. Following an annotation task to select the seed words from FrameNet (Baker et al., 1998), WordNet relations are exploited to expand the sensory seed synsets that are acquired by mapping the seed words to WordNet synsets. At each bootstrapping cycle, a five-class sensorial classifier model is constructed over the seed synsets defined by their WordNet glosses. The expansion continues until the prediction performance of the model steadily drops.

In the second phase, a corpus based method is utilized to estimate the association scores in the final lexicon. Each entry in the lexicon consists of a lemma and part-of-speech (POS) tag pair and their associations to the five human senses (i.e. sight, hearing, taste, smell and touch) measured in terms of normalized pointwise mutual information (NPMI). Each sensorial association provided by the lexicon is a float value in the range of -1 and 1.

Due to the way it is constructed, Sensicon might tend to give high association values for metaphorical sense associations of words as well as the literal ones. For instance, while adjective *dark* is related to *sight* as the literal sense association, Sensicon assigns very high association values to both *sight* and *taste*. While this tendency would be helpful as a hint for identifying synaesthetic words, metaphor identification task would need a complementary word-sense association resource that could highlight the literal sense association of a word.

3.2 Dependency-parsed corpus (DPC)

As an alternative to *Sensicon* for building word-sense associations, we extract this information from a corpus of dependency-parsed sentences. To achieve that, we follow a similar approach to Özbal et al. (2014) and use a database that stores, for each relation in the dependency treebank of LDC GigaWord 5th Edition corpus[5]), its occurrences with specific "governors" (heads) and "dependents" (modifiers). To determine the sensorial load of a noun n, we first count how many times n occurs with the verb lemmas 'see', 'smell', 'hear', 'touch' and 'taste' in a direct object (*dobj*) syntactic relation in the database. Then, we divide each count by the number of times n appears in a direct object syntactic relation independently of the head that it is connected to. More specifically, the probability that n is associated to sense s is calculated as:

$$\mathrm{p}(s,n) = \frac{\mathrm{c}_{dobj}(v_s, n)}{\sum_{h_i} \mathrm{c}_{dobj}(h_i, n)} \tag{1}$$

where $c_r(h,m)$ is the number of times that m depends on h in relation r (in this case, $r = dobj$) in the dependency database, v_s is the most representative verb for sense s (e.g., the verb 'hear' for the sense of hearing) and each h_i is a different governor of n in a *dobj* relation as observed in the database.

[5] http://www.ldc.upenn.edu/Catalog/catalogEntry.jsp?catalogId=LDC2011T07

Our hypothesis is that nouns frequently acting as a direct object of a verb representing a human sense s are highly associated to s.

Similarly, to extract the sensorial load of an adjective a, we calculate the number of times a occurs with the verb lemmas 'look', 'smell', 'sound', 'feel' and 'taste' in an adjectival complement (*acomp*) syntactic relation in the database. Then, we divide each count by the number of times a appears in an *acomp* syntactic relation. More specifically, the probability that a is associated to sense s is calculated as:

$$\mathrm{p}(s,a) = \frac{\mathrm{c}_{acomp}(v_s, a)}{\sum_{h_i} \mathrm{c}_{acomp}(h_i, a)} \tag{2}$$

The two resources capture different properties of words with respect to their sensorial load. While Sensicon yields indirect sensorial associations by modeling distributional properties of the lexicon, DPC attempts to directly model these associations independently of the context. For instance, while Sensicon associates the noun *plate* with *taste* as it frequently occurs in contexts involving eating, DPC assigns the highests scores to *sight* and *touch*.

4 Evaluation

In this section, we demonstrate the impact of sensorial associations of words on the classification of adjective-noun pairs as metaphorical or literal expressions.

4.1 Dataset

As an initial attempt to investigate the impact of sensorial associations of words in metaphor identification, we target metaphorical expressions which can easily be isolated from their context. In this study, we focus on adjective-noun (AN) pairs which could also well suit a common definition of the synaesthetic metaphors as adjective metaphors where an adjective associated to one sense modality describes a noun related to another modality (Utsumi and Sakamoto, 2007). To this end, we experiment with the AN dataset constructed by Tsvetkov et al. (2014a). The dataset consists of literal and metaphorical AN relations collected from public resources on the web and validated by human annotators. For instance, it includes *green energy*, *straight answer* as metaphorical relations and *bloody nose, cool air* as literal relations. To be able to compare our model with the state-of-the-art, we use the same training and test split as Tsvetkov et al. (2014a). More precisely, 884 literal and 884 metaphorical AN pairs are used for training, while 100 literal and 100 metaphorical AN pairs are used for testing.

4.2 Classifier and Features

We perform a literal/metaphorical classification task by adding sensorial features on top of the features proposed by Tsvetkov et al. (2014a), which constitute our baseline: concreteness, imageability, supersenses and vector space word representations. As we discussed earlier, *imageability* (I) and *concreteness* (C) are highly effective in metaphor identification task. We obtain the I and C scores of each word from the resource constructed by Tsvetkov et al. (2014a) by projecting I and C values of words in MRCPD onto 150,114 English words. *Supersenses* are coarse semantic representations that could reflect the conceptual mappings between adjective and noun components of a relation. We attain noun supersenses from the lexicographer files of WordNet, such as *noun.phenomenon, noun.feeling, verb.perception*, and adjective supersenses from the resource generated by Tsvetkov et al. (2014b). As the last baseline feature, *Vector Space Word Representations* can be considered as lexical-semantic properties where each word is represented by a vector and semantically similar words have similar vectors. The detailed description of how the baseline features are extracted can be found in Tsvetkov et al. (2014a).

As the main focus of this study, we extract the sensorial features from Sensicon and a dependency-parsed corpus (DPC). For each adjective and noun in an AN relation, we add as features its five sense associations according to the two resources. This results in 10 features (S) coming from Sensicon and 10 features (D) coming from DPC. From S and D, we derive two more features (p_S and p_D respectively) computed as the Pearson correlation between the sense features for the noun and the adjective.

As the third type of sensorial feature, we add a feature (R) which encodes the degree to which the adjective noun pair is consistent with William's theory of sense modality directionality in synaesthetic metaphors (Williams, 1976). According to Williams, the mapping between the source and target sense of a synaesthetic adjective is more likely to flow in some directions and not in others, as exemplified in Figure 1. For example, while synaesthetic metaphors could be constructed with touch related adjectives and taste related nouns, the opposite direction, a taste related adjective and touch related noun, is less likely to occur. In our study, we employed simplified version of the directionality mapping in Figure 1 by identifying sight modality with *dimension* and *color*. For an AN relation, we first assign a sense to each component (i.e., adjective and noun) by choosing the highest sense association in DPC. We decided to employ DPC instead of Sensicon in the definition of this feature since by construction it provides a more direct association between words and senses. The value of R is set to 1.0 if the sense associations of the adjective and noun satisfies a direction in Figure 1. If the associations violate the directions in the figure, the value of the feature is set to 0.5. In all other cases it is set to 0.

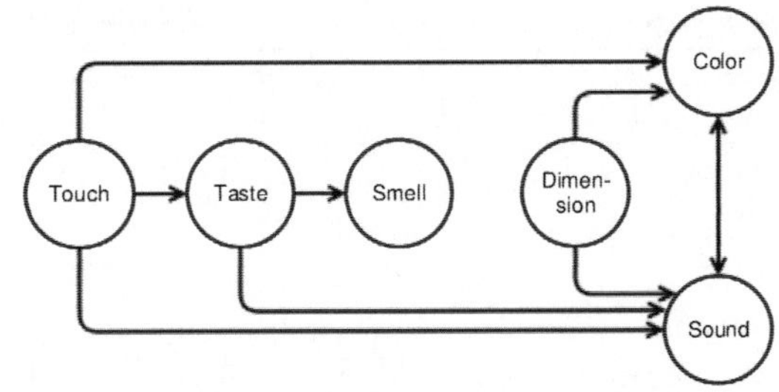

Figure 1: Directionality of sensory modalities as proposed by Williams(1976).

Another sensorial feature set (W) is constructed by checking if the constituents of an AN pair appear in the Sensicon seed set, which consists of 4,287 sensorial words. For each adjective and noun, we add 5 binary features (one for each sense) and if the word is listed among the seeds for a specific sense, the feature for that sense is set to 1. In the same way, we construct another feature set (L) from the resource described in (Lynott and Connell, 2013; Lynott and Connell, 2013). This resource contains 1,000 nouns and object properties annotated with the five senses. Table 1 summarizes the features used in the classification task.

Feature Name	Abbreviation	# of the Features
Baseline	B	183
Baseline - VSM	B'	55
Sensicon	S	10
Sensicon Pearson	p_S	1
DPC	D	10
DPC Pearson	p_D	1
Sensicon Seeds	W	10
Lynott-Connell Sense Words	L	10
Directionality Rules	R	1
All sensorial features	A	43

Table 1: Feature sets used in the experiments.

To replicate the experimental setup of Tsvetkov et al. (2014a) as closely as possible, for our experiment we also use a Random Forest classifier, which was demonstrated to outperform other classification algorithms and to be robust to overfitting (Breiman, 2001). To fine tune the classifier and find the best Random Forest model for each feature set combination, we perform a grid search over the number of the generated trees (in the range between 50 and 300) and the maximum depth of the tree (in the range between 0 and 50) using 10-fold cross validation on AN training data. We choose the best model for each feature combination based on the maximum *average cross validation accuracy - standard deviation* value obtained by applying the given parameters.

4.3 Evaluation of the Baseline Features

The first row in Table 2 demonstrates the accuracy obtained with the complete set of baseline features. As it can be observed from the results, there is a significant drop of accuracy when moving from training to test data. We suspect that this performance loss might be due to the high dimensionality of the vector space feature set. Since according to Tsvetkov et al. (2014a) these features were designed mostly to deal with the multilinguality of their experimental setting, we evaluate the performance of the baseline excluding the vector space features. The row labeled B' reports the resulting accuracy values. The figures show that this simpler model has better generalization performance on monolingual English data. Hence, we decide to add our sensorial features on top of the simplified B' baseline.

Features	Cross-validation	Test
B	0.851	0.798
B'	0.831	0.845

Table 2: The cross validation and test accuracies of the baseline with and without vector space features.

4.4 Evaluation of the Sensorial Features

The second row labeled 'All' in Table 3 shows the cross validation and test accuracies of the sensorial features added on top of B'. The following rows show the outcome of the ablation experiments in which we remove each feature set at a time. The results that are marked with one or more $*$ indicate a statistically significant improvement in comparison to B' according to McNemar's test (McNemar, 1947). From the results it can be observed that the model including all sensorial features outperforms the baseline in both cross-validation and testing even though the difference on test data is not significant.

According to the ablation experiments, sensorial transaction rules (R) yield the highest contribution. While the Pearson correlation value calculated with Sensicon (p_S) results in an improvement, the feature representing the correlation with DPC (p_D) causes a decrease in the performance of the model. In general, all models using any tested subset of the sensorial features outperform the very competitive baseline even though the difference is significant only in two cases. To have more conclusive insights about the importance of each feature, an analysis on a larger dataset would be necessary. Overall, all the results demonstrate the useful contribution of the sensorial features to the task.

4.5 Error Analysis

The analysis that we performed on the test results shows that the noticeable performance differences among test results arise from the number of the instances in the test set. Indeed, a more comprehensive and bigger test set would provide better insights about the performance of sensorial features in the metaphor identification task.

[6] For two classifiers that have the same accuracy, McNemar test can yield different results with respect to the same baseline, depending on the tendency of each classifier to make the same errors as the baseline.

Features	Cross-validation	Test
B'	0.831	0.845
All	0.852**	0.875
All-S	0.850**	0.870
All-D	0.838	0.875
All-p_S	**0.855*****	0.870
All-p_D	0.851**	**0.890***
All-R	0.838	0.865
All-L	0.853**	0.880
All-W	0.853**	0.880*[6]

Table 3: Performance of the B' baseline in combination with the different sets of sensorial features. Statistical significance: ***, $p < .001$; **, $p < .01$; *, $p < .05$.

Regarding the impact of the sensorial features, the test results indicate that sensorial association of the words could be beneficial in resolving the metaphors that include at least one sensorial component. For instance, the best configuration All-p_D could identify the *quiet revolution* as metaphorical while identifying *quiet voice* as literal with the sensorial adjective *quiet*.

A highly observable problem that causes error in the predictions is the limited coverage of the sensorial association resources. As an example, the literal AN pair *woolly mammoth* could not be resolved, since the adjective *woolly*, which is highly related to touch modality, can not be found in either Sensicon or DPC.

As another type of error, for less direct relations to sensory modalities, DPC might not provide the right information. For instance, in the literal AN relation *blind man*, the adjective *blind* is associated with taste as the highest sensory relation while associating man with sight modality. This might lead to the classification of this literal pair as metaphorical.

Considering the shortcomings of the current sensorial resources, a better sensorial lexicon differentiating various aspects of sensorial words such as direct sensorial properties (e.g., *coldness*, *odor* or *touch*), perceptibility of the concepts such as the visible concept (e.g., *cloud*), or tasteable concept (e.g., *food*), and also deeper cognitive relations of the words with senses such as *microphone* with hearing or *blind* with sight, could increase the performance of the metaphor identification systems.

5 Conclusion

In this paper, we investigated the impact of sensorial features on the identification of metaphors in the form of adjective-noun pairs. We adopted a lexical approach for feature extraction in the same vein as the other cognitive features employed in metaphor identification, such as imageability and concreteness. To this end, we first utilized a state-of-the-art lexicon (i.e. *Sensicon*) associating English words to sensorial modalities. Then, we proposed a novel technique to automatically discover these associations from a dependency-parsed corpus. In our experiments, we evaluated the contribution of the sensorial features to the task when added to a state-of-the art model. Our results demonstrate that sensorial features are beneficial for the task and they generalize well as the accuracy improvements observed on the training data constantly reflect on test performance. To the best of our knowledge, this is the first model explicitly using sensorial features for metaphor detection. We believe that our results should encourage the community to explore further ways to encode sensorial information for the task and possibly to also use such features for other NLP tasks.

As future work, we would like to investigate the impact of sensorial features on the classification of other metaphor datasets such as VU Amsterdam Metaphor Corpus (Steen et al., 2010) and TroFi (Trope Finder) Example Base[7]. It would also be interesting to explore the contribution of these features for other figure of speech types such as similes. Furthermore, we plan to extend DPC approach with the automatic discovery of sensorial associations of verbs and adverbs in addition to adjectives and nouns. These efforts could result in the compilation of a new sensorial lexicon.

Acknowledgements

We would like to thank Daniele Pighin for reviewing our paper, his insightful comments and valuable suggestions.

[7] Available at http://www.cs.sfu.ca/anoop/students/jbirke/

References

Collin F Baker, Charles J Fillmore, and John B Lowe. 1998. The berkeley framenet project. pages 86–90. Association for Computational Linguistics.

Beata Beigman Klebanov, Ben Leong, Michael Heilman, and Michael Flor. 2014. Different texts, same metaphors: Unigrams and beyond. In *Proceedings of the Second Workshop on Metaphor in NLP*, pages 11–17, Baltimore, MD, June. Association for Computational Linguistics.

Julia Birke and Anoop Sarkar. 2006. A clustering approach for nearly unsupervised recognition of nonliteral language. In *EACL*.

Leo Breiman. 2001. Random forests. *Machine learning*, 45(1):5–32.

George Aaron Broadwell, Umit Boz, Ignacio Cases, Tomek Strzalkowski, Laurie Feldman, Sarah Taylor, Samira Shaikh, Ting Liu, Kit Cho, and Nick Webb. 2013. Using imageability and topic chaining to locate metaphors in linguistic corpora. In *Social Computing, Behavioral-Cultural Modeling and Prediction*, pages 102–110. Springer.

Max Coltheart. 1981. The mrc psycholinguistic database. *The Quarterly Journal of Experimental Psychology*, 33(4):497–505.

Dan Fass. 1991. met*: A method for discriminating metonymy and metaphor by computer. *Computational Linguistics*, 17(1):49–90.

Matt Gedigian, John Bryant, Srini Narayanan, and Branimir Ciric. 2006. Catching metaphors. In *Proceedings of the Third Workshop on Scalable Natural Language Understanding*, pages 41–48. Association for Computational Linguistics.

Dirk Hovy, Shashank Srivastava, Sujay Kumar Jauhar, Mrinmaya Sachan, Kartik Goyal, Huiying Li, Whitney Sanders, and Eduard Hovy. 2013. Identifying metaphorical word use with tree kernels. *Meta4NLP 2013*, page 52.

George Lakoff and Mark Johnson. 1980. *Metaphors We Live By*. University of Chicago press.

Dermot Lynott and Louise Connell. 2013. Modality exclusivity norms for 400 nouns: The relationship between perceptual experience and surface word form. *Behavior research methods*, 45(2):516–526.

Quinn McNemar. 1947. Note on the sampling error of the difference between correlated proportions or percentages. *Psychometrika*, 12(2):153–157, jun.

Michael Mohler, David Bracewell, David Hinote, and Marc Tomlinson. 2013. Semantic signatures for example-based linguistic metaphor detection. *Meta4NLP 2013*, page 27.

Yair Neuman, Dan Assaf, Yohai Cohen, Mark Last, Shlomo Argamon, Newton Howard, and Ophir Frieder. 2013. Metaphor identification in large texts corpora. *PloS one*, 8(4):e62343.

Gözde Özbal, Daniele Pighin, and Carlo Strapparava. 2014. Automation and evaluation of the keyword method for second language learning. In *Proceedings of the 52nd Annual Meeting of the Association for Computational Linguistics (Volume 2: Short Papers)*, pages 352–357. Association for Computational Linguistics.

Mario Pricken. 2008. *Creative Advertising Ideas and Techniques from the World's Best Campaigns*. Thames & Hudson, 2nd edition.

Marc Schulder and Eduard Hovy. 2014. Metaphor detection through term relevance. *ACL 2014*, page 18.

Yeshayahu Shen. 1997. Cognitive constraints on poetic figures. *Cognitive Linguistics (includes Cognitive Linguistic Bibliography)*, 8(1):33–72.

Ekaterina Shutova and Lin Sun. 2013. Unsupervised metaphor identification using hierarchical graph factorization clustering. In *HLT-NAACL*, pages 978–988.

Ekaterina Shutova, Lin Sun, and Anna Korhonen. 2010. Metaphor identification using verb and noun clustering. In *Proceedings of the 23rd International Conference on Computational Linguistics*, pages 1002–1010. Association for Computational Linguistics.

Gerard J Steen, Aletta G Dorst, J Berenike Herrmann, Anna A Kaal, and Tina Krennmayr. 2010. Metaphor in usage. *Cognitive Linguistics*, 21(4):765–796.

Serra Sinem Tekiroglu, Gözde Özbal, and Carlo Strapparava. 2014. Sensicon: An automatically constructed sensorial lexicon. In *Proceedings of the 2014 Conference on Empirical Methods in Natural Language Processing (EMNLP)*, pages 1511–1521, Doha, Qatar, October. Association for Computational Linguistics.

Yulia Tsvetkov, Leonid Boytsov, Anatole Gershman, Eric Nyberg, and Chris Dyer. 2014a. Metaphor detection with cross-lingual model transfer. In *Proceedings of the 52nd Annual Meeting of the Association for Computational Linguistics*, pages 248–258. Association for Computational Linguistics.

Yulia Tsvetkov, Nathan Schneider, Dirk Hovy, Archna Bhatia, Manaal Faruqui, and Chris Dyer. 2014b. Augmenting english adjective senses with supersenses. In *Proc. of LREC*.

Peter D Turney, Yair Neuman, Dan Assaf, and Yohai Cohen. 2011. Literal and metaphorical sense identification through concrete and abstract context. In *Proceedings of the 2011 Conference on the Empirical Methods in Natural Language Processing*, pages 680–690.

Shimon Ullman. 1957. Panchronistic tendencies in synaesthesia. *The principles of semantics*, pages 266–289.

Akira Utsumi and Maki Sakamoto. 2007. Computational evidence for two-stage categorization as a process of adjective metaphor comprehension. In *Proceedings of the Second European Cognitive Science Conference (EuroCogSci2007)*, pages 77–82.

Joseph M Williams. 1976. Synaesthetic adjectives: A possible law of semantic change. *Language*, pages 461–478.

MetaNet: Deep semantic automatic metaphor analysis

Ellen Dodge and Jisup Hong
International Computer Science Institute
1947 Center Street Ste. 600
Berkeley, CA 94704
edodge@icsi.berkeley.edu
jhong@icsi.berkeley.edu

Elise Stickles
University of California, Berkeley
1203 Dwinelle Hall
Berkeley, CA 94720-2650
elstickles@berkeley.edu

Abstract

This paper describes a system that makes use of a repository of formalized frames and metaphors to automatically detect, categorize, and analyze expressions of metaphor in corpora. The output of this system can be used as a basis for making further refinements to the system, as well as supporting deep semantic analysis of metaphor expressions in corpora. This in turn provides a way to ground and test empirical conceptual metaphor theory, as well as serving as a means to gain insights into the ways conceptual metaphors are expressed in language.

1 Introduction

Recognition of the ubiquity of metaphor in language has led to increased interest in automatic identification of metaphoric expressions in language. Typical approaches to metaphor analysis in linguistics comprise (a) theory-driven introspective top-down methods, and (b) bottom-up corpus approaches with an emphasis on analyzing how metaphors are used in discourse. Computational approaches tend to focus on the task of metaphor detection (i.e. determining whether a particular expression metaphoric or not) rather than attempting to identify and analyze which conceptual metaphors are being expressed.

The MetaNet approach described here bridges the two linguistic methodologies above by providing (a) a linguist-friendly interface for formally representing conceptual metaphor theoretic analyses and principles, and (b) an automatic metaphor detection system that applies those analyses and principles to identify metaphoric expressions within large-scale corpora. What results is an integrated system that connects the output of the metaphor detection process to rich information that enables further semantic analysis. This serves as a means for advancing and refining conceptual metaphor theory, and increasing our understanding of how metaphors are used in language.

1.1 Related work

Our work addresses two important criticisms that have been directed toward much previous linguistic work in conceptual metaphor analysis. One issue is that such analyses are often idiosyncratic, with methods of analysis and representations of metaphor varying from analyst to analyst; to address this, metaphor study needs rigorous methodological analyses that can be replicated (Pragglejaz 2007, Kövecses 2011). Another criticism is that metaphor theorists often take a top-down approach that relies on analysis of data gathered from introspection; this tends to limit discovery of new metaphors, and focus analysis on those metaphors the analyst has already identified or vetted from the literature. This contrasts with a bottom-up, corpus-based approach espoused by Stefanowitsch (2006), Deignan (2005), Martin (2006), and others, who argue that identifying as many metaphors as possible in a corpus leads to a clearer picture of the full inventory of metaphoric expressions, as well as providing a measure of their relative frequency of use. Furthermore, such a method can serve to verify theories based on previously-identified metaphors, as well as aiding the discovery of previously-unidentified metaphors.

Various computational approaches have been applied to the task of metaphor detection. Among the first systems, Fass (1991) used selectional pref-

Proceedings of the Third Workshop on Metaphor in NLP, pages 40–49,
Denver, Colorado, June 5, 2015.

erence violations as a cue for nonliteralness, and then relied on comparisons to a knowledge base for further disambiguation. Gedigian et al. (2006)'s system achieved high accuracy at classifying verbs in PropBank annotated texts, though only from a limited domain for a small range of source domain frames, using features consisting of the verb plus its argument filler types expressed as WordNet synsets. In a larger-scale system, Shutova et al. (2010) used unsupervised clustering methods to create noun and verb clusters that represent target and source concepts, respectively. Mappings between them, established by metaphoric seed expressions, were then used to generate novel target-source expressions. Similarly, Mohler et al. (2013)'s system builds semantic signatures that map text to areas in a multidimensional conceptual space and represent associations between concepts. These are compared to known metaphoric ones to detect novel metaphoric expressions. Other systems, such as Turney et al. (2011) and Tsvetkov et al. (2014) determine metaphoricity based on lexical features such as abstractness/concreteness, imageability, and supersenses derived from WordNet.

Our approach to metaphor detection differs from previous approaches in its deliberate dependence on formalization of a particular theory of metaphor and the correctness and completeness of a conceptual metaphor repository expressed in that formalism. By design, we expect the system to succeed at identifying metaphoric expressions to the extent that the formalism and the repository are consistent and correct. The approach thus integrates top-down linguistic and bottom-up computational approaches to metaphor identification and annotation, combining the strengths of each. A significant outcome is that in addition to detecting metaphors in text, our system also yields semantic information about each of these expressions, including identification of source and target domains and links to underlying conceptual metaphors.

1.2 System overview

There are three key components in our system: (1) a repository of formalized metaphors, frames, metaphor constructions, and metaphoric relational patterns; (2) an automated metaphor extraction system that utilizes information from the repository to identify expressions of metaphor in text and annotate them for additional semantic information; and (3) computational tools to evaluate, analyze, and visualize the extracted metaphor data. Together, these are used to form a 'cycle' of analysis, in which analysis of extracted data serves as a means to refine and expand the repository, which in turn improves metaphor extraction results. The system is currently in development for analysis of American English, Mexican Spanish, and Russian.

2 Improvements to Extraction Based on Formalization of Metaphor Theory

Since Lakoff and Johnson's first book on conceptual metaphor theory (1980), the field has come to recognize the hierarchical and taxonomic nature of metaphors and the concepts that comprise their source and target domains. For example, consider the phrases *poverty infects society* and *crime is plaguing the nation*, which instantiate the specific metaphors POVERTY IS A DISEASE and CRIME IS A DISEASE, respectively. However, they inherit much of their semantics from a more general metaphor, SOCIAL PROBLEMS ARE AFFLICTIONS; this in turn inherits from a yet more general metaphor, NEGATIVELY EVALUTED CONDITIONS ARE PHYSICALLY HARMFUL, as shown in Figure 1.

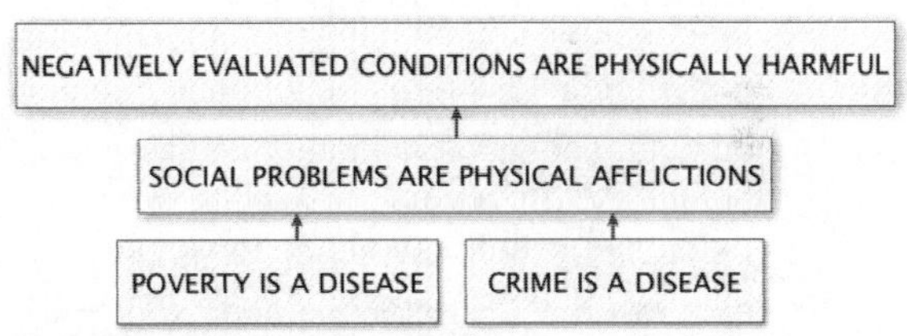

Figure 1. Metaphor inheritance network

It is also clear that the semantic domains of these metaphors are themselves hierarchically related: poverty and crime are social problems, which are negative conditions; meanwhile, disease is a type of physical affliction, which in turn is something that causes physical harm. These domains are represented in our system as semantic frames (Fillmore 1976) similar to those instantiated in FrameNet (Ruppenhofer et al., 2010), which constitute conceptual gestalts that describe particular situations or events along with their participants and other basic conceptual structures. By developing a system that formally represents these structures and relations in an ontology of frames and metaphors, we enable the possibility of a rigorous system of representation that can be computationally implemented and leveraged for improved metaphor detection.

2.1 Repository of metaphors and frames

The MetaNet project represents an effort to formally represent and categorize metaphors and frames that comprise their source and target domains, and relations between them. Frames are coherent, conceptual gestalts organized in a hierarchical structure. These range from experiential universal structures such as Motion Along a Path and Verticality, to more specific situations such as Physical Restraints and Disease; they also include less physically concrete culturally-based frames like Poverty and Corruption. More-specific frames incorporate the semantics and internal structure of the more-general frames they inherit from, forming a complex network of related concepts. Relations between frames define how elements of a parent frame are incorporated by the child frame. For instance, the 'subcase of' relation indicates that the child fully inherits and elaborates the structure of the parent frame. In addition to traditional ontological relations, we also include relations specific to frame semantics and metaphor theory. A fragment of this network is illustrated in Figure 2.

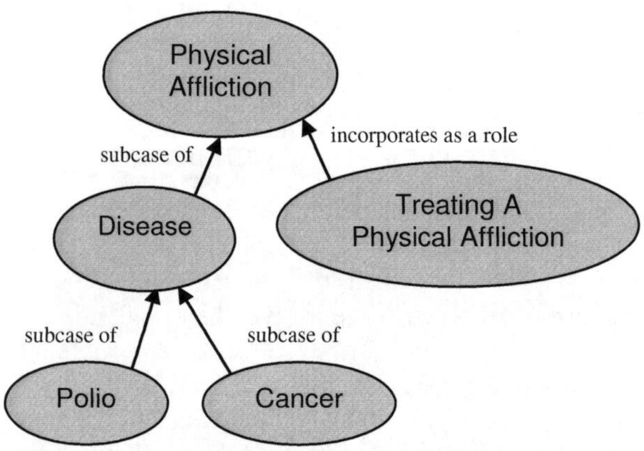

Figure 2. Non-metaphoric frame network pattern

Sub-networks like the group of Physical Affliction frames in Figure 2 are further grouped together to form families of frames, which define collections of broader, but still coherent, conceptual domains.

In addition to relations between frames, structure within frames is also represented in the repository. This includes such elements as participant roles, aspectual and causal structures, relationships between roles, and lexical units that evoke the frame. Figure 3 illustrates partial frame representations of the Poverty and Disease frames. Internal frame structure not only enables improved analysis by requiring the analyst to consider the details of each frame, but also provides additional information in metaphor detection. As the detection system identifies the frames that contribute to the identified metaphor, the detailed semantics of those concepts can be accessed via these frame entries.

Metaphors are essentially representations of mappings between frames. The structure of the source domain frame maps onto the structure of the target domain frame (Figure 3); hence, in POVERTY IS A DISEASE, the *impoverished people* of the Poverty frame are understood as the *patient* experiencing the disease in the Disease frame. Specifically, the roles of the Disease frame map onto their counterparts of the Poverty frame.

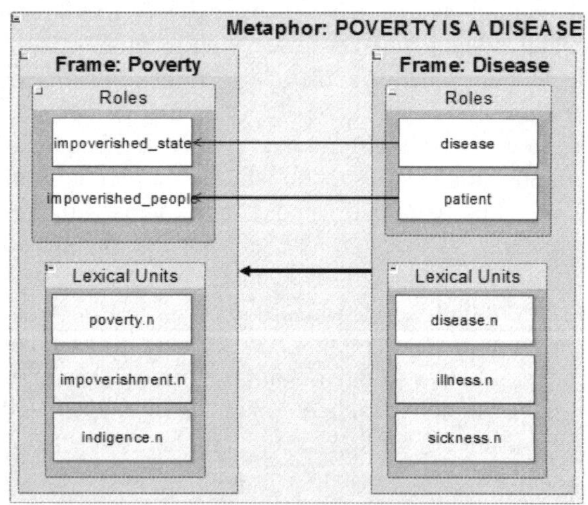

Figure 3. Metaphor structure

Furthermore, just as frame-frame relations define how one frame incorporates the semantics of another, metaphor-metaphor relations define the hierarchy of metaphors (Figure 1). The result is a complex, lattice-like inheritance network of concepts and metaphors.

The computational architecture used for this purpose is a Wiki, based on the Semantic Mediawiki format (Krötzsch et al. 2006). Linguists trained in conceptual metaphor theory create frame and metaphor entries as individual pages, specifying for each metaphor its source and target domain frames, role-to-role mappings, and relations between that metaphor and others in a network. Initially the repository was seeded from metaphors previously identified in the past 30 years of metaphor literature; including comprehensive analysis of primary metaphors provides broad coverage of conceptual metaphors that are applicable to many target domains. For example, the metaphor MORE IS UP can be found in such varied expressions as *prices skyrocketed, she had high hopes,* and *studying boosted his GPA.* Following this initial stage, additional metaphors are added as analysts find them via focused study of particular target domains; however, the system can identify metaphoric language even in the absence of specific metaphors by utilizing the frame network to find more general-level metaphors, as will be shown in section 3.2.

2.2 Metaphor constructions

Previous research has demonstrated that metaphors tend to be expressed in certain regular constructional patterns (Croft 2002; Sullivan 2007, 2013). For example, the noun phrase *poverty trap* has the source domain lexeme *trap* modified by the target domain lexeme *poverty*; these noun-noun metaphor constructions consistently appear in this dependency relation. In contrast, the reverse construction with the source modifying the target is not observed in corpus data (Sullivan 2013). Building on this research, our project has defined a set of grammatical constructions that represent several different types of frequently occurring patterns. In each, the construction specifies which constructional element evokes the source domain, and which evokes the target domain (Table 1). The source term fills different slots in these various patterns; the source may appear not only as a verb, but also as a noun or adjective. As described in section 3.1, these constructions enable us to link a broad range of potentially metaphoric expressions (e.g. lexical units, expressed in some constructional pattern) to the frames and conceptual metaphors in our repository. However, while this process eliminates much data that is *not* metaphoric, it does not positively identify expressions that *are* metaphoric: for example, the same noun-noun pattern that identifies *poverty trap* also returns the literal expression *bear trap.* Hence, disambiguating between these two types of expressions requires a second step of metaphoricity evaluation.

Constructional pattern	**Examples**
T-subj_S-verb	*poverty infects*
T-subj_S-verb-conj	*poverty infects and maims*
T-subj-conj_S-verb	*homelessness and poverty infect*
S-verb_T-dobj	*escape poverty*
S-verb_T-dobj-conj	*escape despair and poverty*
S-verb_Prep_T-noun	*slide into poverty / pull up out of poverty*
S-noun_of_T-noun	*trap of poverty*
T-noun_poss_S-noun	*poverty's undertow*
S-noun_prep_T-noun	*path to poverty*
T-noun_mod_S-noun	*poverty trap*
S-adj_mod_T-noun	*burdensome poverty*
T-noun_cop_S-noun-adj	*poverty is a disease / poverty is burdensome*

Table 1. Constructional Patterns

3 Metaphor Extraction and Identification

Our automatic metaphor identification system divides into two main phases. In the first, we use a set of manually defined metaphoric constructional patterns to identify candidate expressions with explicitly realized potential target and source elements. In the second, we identify the frames that are evoked by these elements, and use our conceptual network of frames and metaphors, along with a set of patterns of relationships between nodes in the network, to determine the likelihood of a candidate expression being metaphoric. These phases are presented in detail below.

3.1 Matching constructional patterns

The first step in the process is to identify potentially metaphoric expressions in the corpus; the system can search for metaphors for a particular target domain family, metaphors that make use of a particular source domain family, or simply all the metaphoric expressions in the data. This search is performed by making use of the metaphoric constructional patterns as described in section 2.2. They are represented as SPARQL queries that specify document structural constraints, including grammatical constraints. To search texts for constructional matches, we construct Resource Description Framework (RDF) models of each sentence in terms of an ontology defined in the Web Ontology Language (OWL). The ontology defines the classes Document, Sentence, and Word, and properties, some of which are shown in Table 2 and with their domain and range.

	Domain	Range
`inDocument`	Sentence	Document
`inSentence`	Word	Sentence
`follows`	Word	Word
`precedes`	Word	Word
`dep`	Word	Word
`hasIdx`	Sentence,Word	integer
`hasForm`	Word	string
`hasLemma`	Word	string
`hasPOS`	Word	string

Table 2. Document properties

The resulting RDF representation of the input text constitutes a graph structure in which words, sentences, and documents are nodes in the graph. Properties serve to characterize nodes in terms of string or integer information, such as form, lemma, part of speech (POS), or position, as well as in terms of a node's relation to other nodes. Such relations, with respect to Word nodes, include ordering relations and grammatical dependency relations. While Table 2 shows only the root of the dependency relations, `dep`, the ontology includes a grammatical relations hierarchy that represents a merger of the hierarchies used by the Stanford (De Marneffe et al., 2006), RASP (Briscoe et al., 2006), and Spanish Freeling (Lloberes et al., 2010) dependency parsers.

Generating this representation requires that NLP tools such as lemmatizers, POS taggers, and dependency parsers be available for the language in question. Because dependency parsing is the most computationally expensive step in this process, in cases where the metaphor extraction is being run only for certain target or source domains, a preprocessing step identifies sentences of interest based on the presence of a word from those domains.

In order to search large volumes of text using SPARQL constructional pattern queries, documents are converted to RDF and uploaded to an OpenRDF Sesame triplestore. Constructional pattern matching queries are run in succession over each document, with queries written so that each match result includes a sentence index, as well as the lemma and word index of the potentially metaphoric lexical elements. Documents are processed in parallel to the extent possible given hardware limitations. With six compute servers each providing 16 cores and running a local triplestore, we were able to run metaphor detection on a preprocessed 500 million word subset of the English Gigaword corpus (Graff & Cieri 2003) in 6 hours.

3.2 Evaluating metaphoricity

The preceding phase of the metaphor extractor returns pairs of words that are related to each other by a constructional pattern where one word may be the source domain of a metaphor, and the other word may be the target domain of that metaphor. While the constructional patterns represent a necessary constraint on metaphoric expression, they are not sufficient to guarantee metaphoricity. Hence, the second phase of metaphor detection makes use of the network of frames and metaphors instantiated in the metaphor repository in order to disambiguate between metaphoric and non-metaphoric expressions in the pool of candidates.

The content of the wiki repository (as described in Section 2.1) is converted to an RDF representation, also in terms of an OWL-defined ontology, and loaded into a triplestore repository. Entries for candidate lexical items in the repository are associated with the frames that they evoke; if the lexical items for English are not already present in the system, FrameNet (https://framenet.icsi.berkeley.edu), WordNet (https://wordnet.princeton.edu), and Wiktionary (https://www.wiktionary.org) data are used to expand the search for the most relevant frame present in the system. After these frames are identified, the system performs searches through the network to determine how the frames are related to one another. If a repository search of the chain of relations that connect the frames includes codified metaphoric mappings, the extractor recognizes the candidate expression as metaphoric.

The likelihood that an expression is metaphoric is determined by attempting to match the relational network between the two frames against a set of pre-defined patterns, which are expressed in

SPARQL and stored in the Semantic MediaWiki, along with the constructional patterns. These patterns fall into two basic types.

The first type are relational configurations that constitute negative evidence for metaphoricity—i.e. they suggest that the expression is not metaphoric. For example, if the potential source and target lexical units evoke the same frame, the system could conclude that the expression is not metaphoric. Similarly, the system can also disregard cases where the frames are too closely related at some point in the network, e.g., if the candidate target lemma evokes a frame that is inherited by the candidate source frame. For example, in the phrases *to cure a disease* and *to cure polio*, *cure* evokes the Treating a Physical Affliction frame, in which one of the roles is the physical affliction being treated. The potential target lemmas *disease* and *polio* evoke the Disease and Polio frames, which inherit from Physical Affliction as shown in Figure 2. The constructional pattern matching phase of the system would identify the expressions as candidates, with *cure* as the source word in both cases, and with *disease* and *polio* as the target words for each phrase. The system, however, is able to exclude these on the basis of a rule that defines a known non-metaphoric network pattern, `TargetIsRoleInSource`, where the frame evoked by the potential target term either directly or recursively inherits from a frame that is incorporated as a role into the frame evoked by the potential source term.

The second type of network relational patterns are a set of rules that constitute positive evidence for metaphoricity. For example, if the two lemmas evoke frames that are defined as target and source frames of a specific conceptual metaphor in the network, then that expression is positively evaluated as a metaphor.

However, it is not necessary that the evoked frames are immediately related to a metaphor entry in the repository. It is not unusual for specific metaphoric mappings not to be present in the conceptual network. This can be due to practical limitations as is often the case with manually created resources, or for principled reasons—for example, in cases where specific metaphors can be predicted from general ones, or for novel extensions that can be interpreted using general metaphors. In those cases, the system is often still able assess metaphoricity on the basis of general mappings defined at a higher level. For example, in the phrase *to cure poverty*, *poverty* evokes the Poverty frame and *cure* the Treating a Physical Affliction frame. In the conceptual network, Poverty is defined as a subcase of Social Problem. Furthermore, Treating a Physical Affliction incorporates the Physical Affliction frame as a role within it. In this case, although the more specific metaphor ADDRESSING POVERTY IS TREATING A DISEASE is not present in the repository network, the system can still identify the candidate pair *cure poverty* as metaphoric on the basis of the higher-level metaphoric mapping SOCIAL PROBLEMS ARE PHYSICAL AFFLICTIONS, as illustrated in Figure 4.

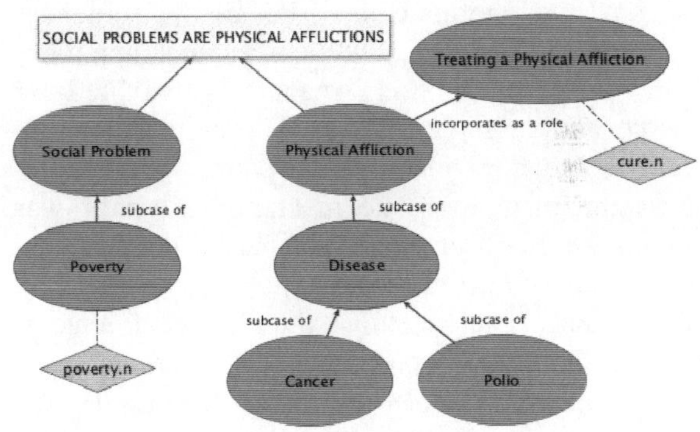

Figure 4. Structures accessed by phrase *cure poverty*.

Consequently, the system is often able to be resilient in the case of specific level gaps in the conceptual network as in the example above.

In addition, the relational patterns are assigned scores that represent the level of confidence that a linguistic expression with a matching frame and metaphor network pattern would actually be metaphoric or non-metaphoric. These scores are used to produce a metaphoricity score for each candidate expression. Although the scores presently assigned to the relational patterns are based on intuition, plans are underway to determine them empirically.

4 Analysis and Evaluation of Data

The extraction process generates a set of annotated sentences that can be used to both evaluate and refine the system, and to perform various kinds of corpus-based analysis. Annotation information includes the lemma, POS, frame, and frame family for both the source and the target terms, as well as the name of the conceptual metaphor identified during the metaphor evaluation process. The purpose for which the extraction is being performed will affect which types of input are used (gold standard data vs. corpora).

4.1 System evaluation and improvements using gold standard

To evaluate the accuracy of the metaphor extractor, linguists collected attested sentences and annotated metaphoric expressions for the target domains Government, Bureaucracy, Democracy, Poverty, Taxation, and Wealth; they annotated all in-domain metaphoric expressions in the sentences where both the target and source were explicitly realized. Sentences were manually annotated for source and target word forms, source and target frames, and the constructional pattern used to express the metaphor. The metaphor extractor was run on these collected gold standard sentences, and the output compared to the annotations entered by the linguists. Table 3 shows the number of annotations in the gold standard, the recall (percentage of gold standard examples that were identified), and the precision (percentage of extracted examples that were correct) of the system for three languages.

Lang.	Anno.	Recall	Precision
English	301	0.86 (258/301)	0.85 (258/305)
Spanish	122	0.88 (107/122)	0.86 (107/125)
Russian	148	0.41 (60/148)	0.90 (60/67)

Table 3. Performance over gold standard data

As shown in Table 3, the system exhibits significantly lower recall for Russian than for the other languages. One of the reasons for this is that our instantiation of the conceptual network of frames and metaphors is not as well developed for Russian as for English and Spanish, containing significantly fewer metaphors and frames, as well as lexical units (LUs) which belong to them.[1] For example, Table 4 below shows the number of metaphors, frames, LUs, and the total number of frame-frame relations of the types used for metaphoricity evaluation. These relations include 'incorporates as a role,' 'subcase of,' and 'makes use of.'

	Metaphors	Frames	LUs	Rels
English	787	656	4308	838
Spanish	547	467	3521	506
Russian	127	303	1674	273

Table 4. Summary of repository content

It should be noted, however, that all the systems, including Russian, identified metaphoric expressions with a high degree of precision. Since the functioning of the metaphor detector depends on the correctness of conceptual metaphor theory, of its formalization in our system, and of the metaphor, frame, constructional pattern, and metaphor relational pattern representations in the repository, this result provides positive indication as to the validity in general of these aspects of the system. The metaphor detector thus in some sense implements the predictions of the formalized theory.

This has the added benefit that results contrary to expectation provide invaluable data for refining the system. For example, it is widely accepted that the government is often conceptualized a kind of physical structure, e.g. *foundation of government*, *the government collapsed overnight*, etc. The metaphor detector, based on representations captured in the repository, searching through a large corpus, turned up volumes of expressions such as *government building* and *government house* that are not metaphoric. This becomes a starting point of investigation to correct some aspect of the content of the repository, of the theory, or of its formalization.

4.2 Corpus-based analysis of metaphor

When corpora are used as input to the extraction system, the extraction results can be used to perform various kinds of corpus-based linguistic analyses. Such analyses can help provide an empirical basis for, and suggest refinements and improvements of, Conceptual Metaphor Theory. For instance, instead of relying on intuitions about how a given target domain is metaphorically conceptualized, it is possible to search a corpus and identify which source domain lemmas and frames are used, and with what relative frequency.

[1] As linguists continue to work on the repository, these numbers will grow.

The richness of the extracted data and the structural relations identified via our repository enable us to analyze data at varying levels of specificity. For instance, a search of the English Gigaword corpus (Graff & Cieri 2003) for metaphor expressions with the target domain 'poverty' revealed several interesting patterns. Firstly, at the very general level of frame families, we observe that the most frequently occurring source terms were either location/motion related (e.g. being at a location, translational motion, motion impediments) or involved physical harm (e.g. disease, physical combat, or other harmful encounters). Figure 5 shows the relative frequency of these frame families.

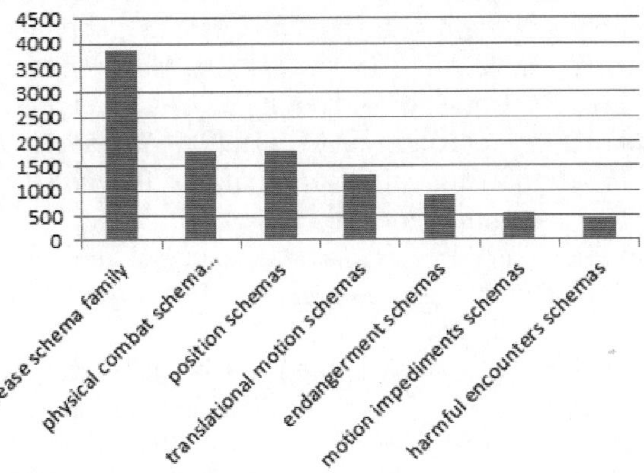

Figure 5. Most frequently occurring source families within poverty data.

At a somewhat more specific level, we can examine which specific frames within one of these families are being evoked. Figure 6 looks within the Translational Motion family, and shows the number of extracted metaphor expressions that evoke each of the frames within that family.

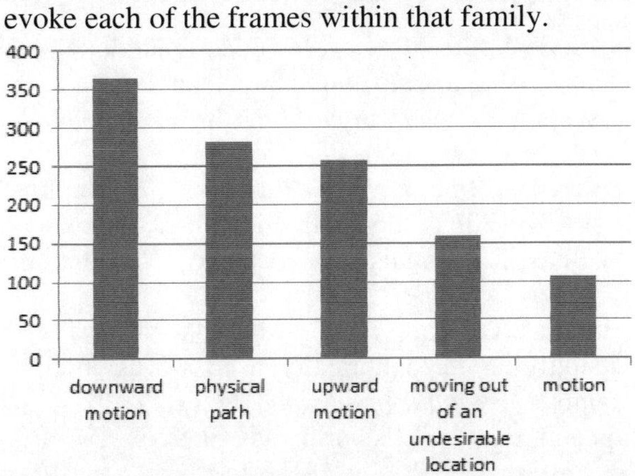

Figure 6. Number of extracted metaphor expressions that evoke various translational motion frames

Looking at a yet more specific level, we can examine which lexical items are used to evoke a given frame. Figure 7, below, shows this data for the Downward Motion frame.

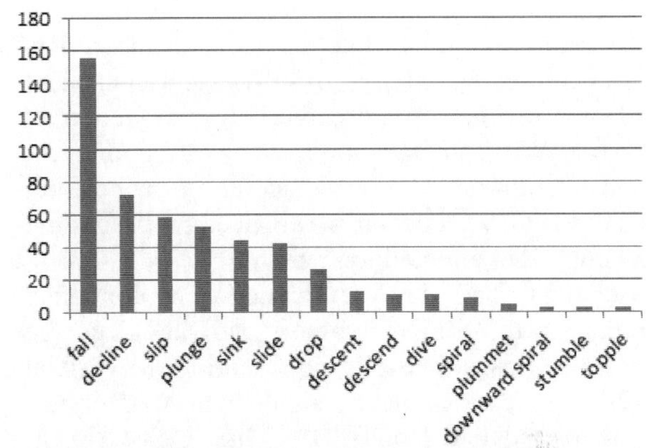

Figure 7. Number of different lexical units in extracted data that evoke the Downward Motion frame.

It is also possible to search for the conceptual metaphor that was discovered during the metaphoricity evaluation phase of the extraction process. For instance, Downward Motion lexemes such as *fall* and *slip* are used in expressions of the conceptual metaphor BECOMING IMPOVERISHED IS MOTION DOWNWARDS (e.g. *the young family fell/slipped into poverty*).

5 Conclusions

Our system moves beyond detection of metaphor, and enables us to perform many kinds of semantic analyses of metaphors in text. This affords the linguistic analyst additional insight into the conceptual structures characteristic of naturally-occurring language. Importantly, the different elements of the system each form part of a cycle, enabling an iterative development process, wherein extracted data informs linguistic analysis, improving the metaphor repository, or the theory, which in turn improves the quality of the extractor output. The resultant MetaNet metaphor repository and the extracted data can serve as valuable resources both for metaphor analysts and for the computational community at large.

Acknowledgments

The MetaNet Analysis and Repository teams: George Lakoff, Eve Sweetser, Oana David, Karie Moorman, Patricia Lichtenstein, Kristina Despot, Luca Gilardi, Collin Baker, Jim Hieronymous, et al.

Supported by the Intelligence Advanced Research Projects Activity (IARPA) via Department of Defense US Army Research Laboratory contract number W911NF-12-C-0022. The U.S. Government is authorized to reproduce and distribute reprints for Governmental purposes notwithstanding any copyright annotation thereon.

Disclaimer: The views and conclusions contained herein are those of the authors and should not be interpreted as necessarily representing the official policies or endorsements, either expressed or implied, of IARPA, DoD/ARL, or the U.S. Government.

References

Briscoe, T., Carroll, J., & Watson, R. (2006, July). The second release of the RASP system. In *Proceedings of the COLING/ACL on Interactive presentation sessions* (pp. 77-80). Association for Computational Linguistics.

Deignan, A. (2005). *Metaphor and corpus linguistics*. Amsterdam/Philadelphia: John Benjamins.

De Marneffe, M. C., MacCartney, B., & Manning, C. D. (2006). Generating typed dependency parses from phrase structure parses. In *Proceedings of LREC* (Vol. 6, No. 2006, pp. 449-454).

Feldman, J., Dodge, E. & Bryant, J. (2009). Embodied Construction Grammar. In Heine B., Narrog H., (eds). *The Oxford Handbook of Linguistic Analysis*. Oxford: Oxford U Press, 111–38.

Fillmore, C. J. 1976. Frame semantics and the nature of language. In Origins and Evolution of Language and Speech, ed. by Stevan R. Harnad, Horst D. Steklis, & Jane Lancaster, 20-32. Annals of the NY Academy of Sciences, Vol. 280.

Graff, D. & Cieri, C. (2003). English Gigaword LDC2003T05. Web Download. Philadelphia: Linguistic Data Consortium.

Kövecses, Z. (2011). Methodological issues in conceptual metaphor theory. In S. Handl & H-J. Schmid (Eds.), *Windows to the Mind: Metaphor, metonymy and conceptual blending* (pp. 23-40). Berlin/New York: Mouton de Gruyter.

Krötzsch, M., Vrandečić, D., & Völkel, M. (2006). Semantic mediawiki. In *The Semantic Web-ISWC 2006* (pp. 935-942). Springer Berlin Heidelberg.

Lakoff, G. (1993). The Contemporary Theory of Metaphor. In A. Ortony (Ed.), *Metaphor and Thought*. Cambridge: Cambridge University Press, 202–251.

Lakoff, G. (1993b). How metaphor structures dreams: The theory of conceptual metaphor applied to dream analysis. *Dreaming*, *3*(2), 77.

Lakoff, G., & Johnson, M. (1980). *Metaphors We Live By*. Chicago: University of Chicago Press.

Lakoff, G., & Johnson, M. (1999). *Philosophy in the flesh: The embodied mind and its challenge to western thought*. Basic books.

Lakoff, G. (2008). The neural theory of metaphor. *The Cambridge handbook of metaphor and thought*, 17-38.

Lakoff, G. (2014). Mapping the brain's metaphor circuitry: metaphorical thought in everyday reason. *Frontiers in Human Neuroscience*, *8*, 958.

Lloberes, M., Castellón, I., & Padró, L. (2010, May). Spanish FreeLing Dependency Grammar. In *LREC* (Vol. 10, pp. 693-699).

Martin J. H.. (2006). "A corpus-based analysis of context effects on metaphor comprehension". In Anatol Stefanowitsch and Stefan Th. Gries (Eds.), *Corpus-Based Approaches to Metaphor and Metonymy* (pp. 214-236). Berlin and New York: Mouton de Gruyter.

Mason, Z. J. (2004). "CorMet: A computational, corpus-based conventional metaphor extraction system." *Computational linguistics*, *30*(1), 23-44.

Mohler, M., Bracewell, D., Hinote, D., & Tomlinson, M. (2013). Semantic signatures for example-based linguistic metaphor detection. *Meta4NLP* 2013, 27.

Pragglejaz Group. (2007). MIP: A method for identifying metaphorically used words in discourse. *Metaphor and Symbol*, *22*(1), 1–39.

Ruppenhofer, J., Ellsworth, M., Petruck, M. R., Johnson, C. R., & Scheffczyk, J. (2010). FrameNet II: Extended theory and practice.

Berkeley, California: International Computer Science Institute
Shutova, E., Sun, L., & Korhonen, A. (2010, August). Metaphor identification using verb and noun clustering. In *Proceedings of the 23rd International Conference on Computational Linguistics* (pp. 1002-1010). Association for Computational Linguistics.
Stefanowitsch, Anatol. (2006). "Words and their metaphors: A corpus-based approach". In Anatol Stefanowitsch and Stefan Th. Gries (Eds.), *Corpus-Based Approaches to Metaphor and Metonymy* (pp. 63-105). Berlin and New York: Mouton de Gruyter.
Sullivan, K. S. (2007). *Grammar in Metaphor: A Construction Grammar Account of Metaphoric Language*. PhD dissertation, University of California Berkeley.
Sullivan, K. S. (2013). *Frames and Constructions in Metaphoric Language*. Amsterdam/Philadelphia: John Benjamins Publishing.
Turney, P. D., Neuman, Y., Assaf, D., & Cohen, Y. (2011). Literal and metaphorical sense identification through concrete and abstract context. In *Proceedings of the 2011 Conference on the Empirical Methods in Natural Language Processing* (pp. 680-690).
Wilks, Y., Galescu, J. A., Allen, J. & Dalton, A. (2013). Automatic Metaphor Detection using Large-Scale Lexical Resources and Conventional Metaphor Extraction. In *Proceedings of the First Workshop on Metaphor in NLP* (pp. 33-44), Atlanta, Georgia, 13 June 2013. Association for Computational Linguistics.

High-Precision Abductive Mapping of Multilingual Metaphors

Jonathan Gordon, **Jerry R. Hobbs**, and **Jonathan May**
Information Sciences Institute
University of Southern California
Marina del Rey, CA
{jgordon,hobbs,jonmay}@isi.edu

Fabrizio Morbini
Institute for Creative Technologies
University of Southern California
Playa Vista, CA
morbini@ict.usc.edu

Abstract

Metaphor is a cognitive phenomenon exhibited in language, where one conceptual domain (the target) is thought of in terms of another (the source). The first level of metaphor interpretation is the mapping of linguistic metaphors to pairs of source and target concepts. Based on the abductive approach to metaphor interpretation proposed by Hobbs (1992) and implemented in the open-source Metaphor-ADP system (Ovchinnikova et al., 2014), we present work to automatically learn knowledge bases to support high-precision conceptual metaphor mapping in English, Spanish, Farsi, and Russian.

1 Introduction

In everyday speech and text, people talk about one conceptual domain (the *target*) in terms of another (the *source*). According to Lakoff and Johnson (1980) and others, these *linguistic metaphors* (LMs) are an observable manifestation of our mental, *conceptual metaphors* (CMs). Computational research on metaphor is important: If natural-language systems treat metaphors at face value, meaning can be missed, resulting in absurd or trivial claims.[1] Additionally, understanding metaphors is a way to recognize the attitudes of different individuals, groups, or cultures. Metaphors express strongly felt emotions (e.g., "I'm *crushed* by taxes"—taxation is a burden or threat) and presupposed understandings of concepts (e.g., "She *won* the argument"—arguments are a form of conflict).

The full interpretation of linguistic metaphors is a difficult problem, but a first level of understanding is the identification of the conceptual source and target domains being invoked. For instance, we can map the linguistic metaphor "fighting poverty" to the ⟨source, target⟩ pair ⟨*War*, *Poverty*⟩.

In this paper, we present work that performs this mapping within the abductive reasoning framework proposed by Hobbs (1992) and implemented by Ovchinnikova et al. (2014). By handling metaphor mapping within a general framework for knowledge-based discourse processing, it is possible to extend conceptual mapping to give deeper analysis, as discussed in section 5. This paper's main contribution is the use of annotated collections of metaphors, describing seven target concepts in terms of 67 source concepts in four languages, to learn the lexical axioms needed for high-precision abductive metaphor mapping.

2 Related Work

Metaphor has been studied extensively in the fields of linguistics, philosophy, and cognitive science (e.g., Lakoff and Johnson, 1980; Lakoff, 1992; Gentner et al., 2002). Computational research on metaphor has focused on the problems of (1) identifying linguistic metaphors in text (e.g., Fass, 1991; Birke and Sarkar, 2006; Shutova et al., 2010; Li and Sporleder, 2010; Tsvetkov et al., 2014) and (2) identifying the source and target concepts invoked by each linguistic metaphor.

[1] Lakoff and Johnson (1980) give the examples, "This theory is made of cheap stucco"—blatantly false—and "Mussolini was an animal"—blatantly true.

Proceedings of the Third Workshop on Metaphor in NLP, pages 50–55,
Denver, Colorado, June 5, 2015.

Knowledge-based approaches to identifying conceptual metaphors include that of Hobbs (1992), described in the following section, KARMA (Narayanan, 1997, 1999), and ATT-Meta (Barnden and Lee, 2002; Agerri et al., 2007). These have relied on the use of manually coded knowledge, limiting their ability to scale across domains and languages.

As an alternative to identifying source and target concepts and, potentially, performing deeper analysis, Shutova (2010) and Shutova et al. (2012) learned literal paraphrases for linguistic metaphors based on co-occurrence frequencies, focusing on LMs consisting only of a verb and its subject or object. E.g., they would rewrite "stir excitement" as "provoke excitement". One limitation of a basic paraphrasing approach to metaphor interpretation is that metaphors do not have fixed interpretations; their meaning is dependent on the discourse context in which they are used.[2]

3 Framework for Metaphor Interpretation

Hobbs et al. (1993) describe an approach to discourse processing based on abductive inference. Abduction is a form of reasoning that, given an observation, produces an explanatory hypothesis. For discourse processing, each sentence is an observation, and the interpretation of the sentence is the best explanation of why the sentence is true given what is already known: commonsense and linguistic knowledge and the content of the discourse up to that point. Hobbs (1992) described the applicability of this approach to the problem of interpreting linguistic metaphors. In this framework, metaphor interpretation is part of the general problem of discourse processing.

Ovchinnikova et al. (2011) presented a semantic discourse processing framework based on abduction, which uses the Mini-Tacitus reasoner (Mulkar et al., 2007) to interpret a sentence by proving its logical form, merging redundancies wherever possible, and making any necessary assumptions. This work was extended by Ovchinnikova et al. (2014) to address the interpretation of metaphor. They presented an end-to-end metaphor interpretation system, going from the recognition of linguistic metaphors in text through to basic natural language explanation of the conceptual metaphor identified by abduction. The effectiveness of this approach was validated by expert linguists for English and Russian metaphors.

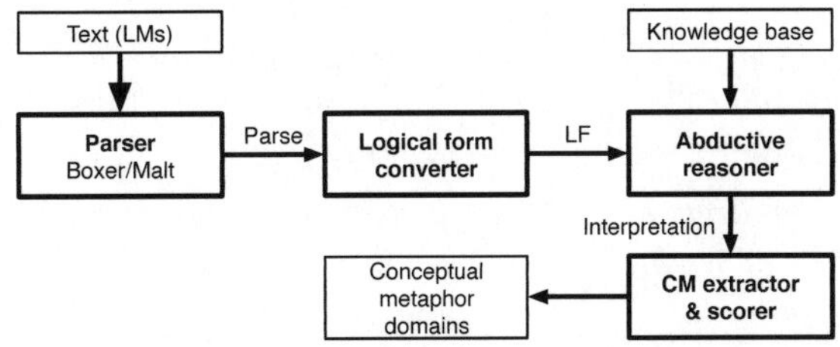

Figure 1: Abduction-based metaphor processing pipeline.

A diagram of the interpretation pipeline is shown in Figure 1. To process a text fragment containing a metaphor, this system generates logical forms (LFs) in the style of Hobbs (1985) by postprocessing the output of the Boxer (Bos et al., 2004) and Malt (Nivre et al., 2006) dependency parsers. A logical form is a conjunction of propositions, where argument links show the relationships among the constituents. An advantage of LFs over the direct use of dependency structures is that they generalize over syntax and they link arguments using long-distance dependencies. While this process is generally reliable, it can result in incorrect part-of-speech suffixes on predicates or inaccurate linking of arguments.

Along with appropriate knowledge bases, the sentential logical forms are input to an engine for weighted abduction based on integer linear programming (Inoue and Inui, 2012). The reasoner finds the most likely (i.e., lowest cost) explanation of the observations (the LF of the text) using knowledge about what conceptual domains explain the use of words and phrases. A conceptual metaphor (CM) extractor and scorer then selects the most likely source–target mappings based on the length of the path linking the source and target in the predicate-argument structure. For this paper, our task consists of the identification of seven target concepts (*Government*, *Democracy*, *Elections*, *Bureaucracy*, *Taxation*, *Poverty*, and *Wealth*) and 67 source concepts used to describe them. A selection of source concepts are listed in Figure 2, and the sizes of the development and test sets annotated with these concepts are given in Table 1.

[2] Hobbs (1992) gives an example: "John is an elephant" should be interpreted as meaning that he is clumsy if it follows "Mary is graceful". In other contexts it might mean that John is large, that he has a good memory, etc.

Abyss	*Container*	*High Location*	*Physical Harm*
Accident	*Contamination*	*Journey*	*Plant*
Animal	*Crime*	*Leader*	*Portal*
Barrier	*Disease*	*Life Stage*	*Protection*
Blood Stream	*Emotion Experiencer*	*Light*	*Resource*
Body of Water	*Enslavement*	*Medicine*	*Science*
Building	*Fire*	*Monster*	*Servant*
Business	*Food*	*Movement*	*Struggle*
Competition	*Forward Movement*	*Obesity*	*Theft*
Confinement	*Game*	*Physical Burden*	*War*

Figure 2: A selection of source concepts.

4 Knowledge Bases and Mapping Performance

The metaphor mapping performance we have achieved is due to two advances over the work of Ovchinnikova et al. (2014): a focus on source and target spans in each sentence and the creation of new knowledge bases. A span is a minimal excerpt of a sentence that is sufficient to mentally trigger the source or target concept. We do not allows spans to overlap or cross sentence boundaries, which may limit our ability to deal with some metaphors. There are one source span and one target span identified per CM, even though a domain might also be supported by words outside the spans. While the spans in our data were annotated manually, they can also be found automatically by LM identification tools like those mentioned in section 2.

We modified the Metaphor-ADP mapping service to filter the logical forms generated by the parser so they only include literals directly related to these spans. We evaluated the contribution of this filtering and found that—for the cross-language average—this improved the precision of source identification significantly with only a small drop in recall:

	Source		Target	
	Prec.	Rec.	Prec.	Rec.
Sentence	39%	22%	84%	49%
Spans	79%	21%	99%	26%

Concentrating on the identified spans particularly helps with sentences containing multiple lexical items that suggest sources or targets, such as those with more than one distinct metaphor, e.g., "... move forward in advancing gun rights ... [so] gun rights [will] be on a solid foundation." The drop seen in target recall is deceptive: The system only returns a mapping when it identifies both a source and a target concept. By no longer identifying erroneous sources from outside the source span, the system now returns no mapping for many sentences where the target could nonetheless be identified correctly. As source concept mapping is the harder problem, our focus is on improving those scores.

Performance at metaphor mapping also depends on the coverage of the knowledge bases (KBs) of *lexical axioms* for each language. These encode information about what words or phrases trigger which source and target concepts. Ovchinnikova et al. (2014) used collections of manually authored axioms for English and Russian, bootstrapped by finding related words and expressions in ConceptNet (Havasi et al., 2007). Manually authoring a knowledge base exploits the intuitions of the knowledge engineer, but these can fail to match the data. In addition, manual enumeration is not a scalable approach to ensure coverage for a wide variety of input LMs.

As such, a further improvement to precision and recall came from work to learn KBs automatically from annotated metaphors. This work sought to automatically generate new axioms from example sentences in our development set by identifying which source and target span words or phrases are most predictive of source and target concepts. We found that as the development sets grow larger, inevitably even those lexical items that seem unambiguous, e.g., "*riqueza*" mapping to the *Wealth* target concept, are ambiguous in our annotations. Sometimes this reflects a real ambiguity (e.g., does "Democrats" relate to *Democracy* or *Elections*?), but it can also be due to erroneous annotations.

	English	Spanish	Farsi	Russian
Dev.	7,963	8,151	7,349	4,851
Test	894	894	881	644

Table 1: The number of metaphoric sentences in the development and test sets for each language.

However, for a goal of high-precision mapping, sophisticated learning methods are not necessary. Instead, we require that a chosen percent of the instances of a logical form fragment correspond to a single source or target concept, in which case we output a lexical axiom mapping the LF to the concept. We found it helpful to enforce the mutual exclusivity of the text fragments that map to source concepts and those that map to target concepts. When a text fragment is ambiguous between a source mapping and a target mapping, we produce an axiom for whichever correspondence was more frequent. This reduces the likelihood of the axioms leading the system to identify, e.g., two source concepts in a sentence but no target concept. The results are axioms like

$$\text{Source:Abyss}(e_0) \Rightarrow \text{bottomless-adj}(e_0, x_0) \wedge \text{pit-nn}(e_1, x_0)$$

If something is described as bottomless and as a pit, an explanation is that it is an instance of the source concept 'Abyss.'

The learned KBs contain approximately twice as many axioms as the manually authored (and bootstrapped) KBs:

	English	Spanish	Farsi	Russian
Manual	1,595	1,024	1,187	1,601
Learned	3,877	2,558	2,481	3,071

Hybrid KBs combining manual and learned axioms yielded the highest recall, at the expense of a loss of precision compared with the automatically learned axioms alone. We would expect manual axioms to perform with higher precision than automatically learned ones. However, this was not so. Learned and hybrid axioms generally outperformed manual ones, as indicated in Table 2. These results could suggest problems with the quality or generality of our manually authored axioms. It is also possible that this demonstrates the consistency of the automatically learned axioms with the annotation of the testing set. E.g., the annotated metaphors used for training and testing sometimes fail to include source concepts that were added later. This can give an advantage in our testing to axioms learned from training data that suffers from the same bias.

	Source		Target	
	Prec.	Rec.	Prec.	Rec.
Manual, Spans	79%	22%	84%	49%
Learned, Spans	85%	56%	99%	65%
Hybrid, Spans	81%	57%	99%	70%

Table 2: Impact of various axiom sources on span-selected Metaphor Mapping performance. Learned and Hybrid approaches generally outperform the Manual approach to axiom collection.

5 Future Work

There are two interesting lines of future work: The first is to devise more refined techniques that are able to take advantage of large dataset of annotated metaphors despite the increase in errors and inconsistencies that normally appear in large collections of annotated data. To this end, we are exploring the use of machine learning techniques to appropriately vary the weights of the learned axioms. The other line of work is to move beyond source and target concept mapping toward a richer interpretation of metaphors.

A target can be viewed differently depending on the role it occupies in a metaphor, which could be handled by axioms such as

$$\text{Source:Physical\_Harm}(e_0) \wedge \text{Role:Threat}(x_0, e_0) \wedge \text{Role:Threatened}(x_1, e_0) \Rightarrow \text{crush-vb}(e_0, x_0, x_1)$$

If something crushes something else, an explanation is that it is a threat causing physical harm to something that is threatened.

where predicates describing general roles related to the source concept are abduced, in addition to the concept itself. By identifying which roles in the source domain are instantiated by target domain elements, we get a more complete picture of the metaphor's meaning. E.g., for the LM "Democracy crushes our dreams", democracy is seen as a threat, while in "Corruption has crushed democracy", it is seen as threatened. The axioms necessary for this interpretation could be manually authored, learned from further annotation of data, or sought by the adaptation of existing work on semantic role labeling.

6 Summary

Understanding the meaning of linguistic metaphors depends, as a first approximation, on the ability to recognize what target concept domain is being discussed in terms of what source concept domain. Within a principled framework for general discourse processing, we have exploited a large body of annotated data to learn knowledge bases for high-precision metaphor mapping.

Acknowledgments

This work was supported by the Intelligence Advanced Research Projects Activity (IARPA) via Department of Defense US Army Research Laboratory contract number W911NF-12-C-0025. The U.S. Government is authorized to reproduce and distribute reprints for Governmental purposes notwithstanding any copyright annotation thereon. Disclaimer: The views and conclusions contained herein are those of the authors and should not be interpreted as necessarily representing the official policies or endorsements, either expressed or implied, of IARPA, DoD/ARL, or the U.S. Government.

References

Rodrigo Agerri, John Barnden, Mark Lee, and Alan Wallington. 2007. Metaphor, inference and domain independent mappings. In Ruslan Mitkov, editor, *Proceedings of the International Conference on Recent Advances in Natural Language Processing (RANLP)*, pages 17–23. Borovets, Bulgaria.

John A. Barnden and Mark G. Lee. 2002. An artificial intelligence approach to metaphor understanding. *Theoria et Historia Scientiarum*, 6(1):399–412.

Julia Birke and Anoop Sarkar. 2006. A clustering approach for nearly unsupervised recognition of nonliteral language. In Diana McCarthy and Shuly Wintner, editors, *Proceedings of the 11th Conference of the European Chapter of the Association for Computational Linguistics (EACL)*, pages 329–36. The Association for Computational Linguistics. Trento, Italy.

Johan Bos, Stephen Clark, Mark Steedman, James R. Curran, and Julia Hockenmaier. 2004. Wide-coverage semantic representations from a CCG parser. In *Proceedings of the 20th International Conference on Computational Linguistics (COLING)*, pages 1240–6. Geneva, Switzerland.

Dan Fass. 1991. met*: A method for discriminating metonymy and metaphor by computer. *Computational Linguistics*, 17(1):49–90.

Dedre Gentner, Mutsumi Imai, and Lera Boroditsky. 2002. As time goes by: Evidence for two systems in processing space–time metaphors. *Language and Cognitive Processes*, 17(5):537–65.

Catherine Havasi, Robert Speer, and Jason Alonso. 2007. ConceptNet 3: A flexible, multilingual semantic network for common sense knowledge. In Ruslan Mitkov, editor, *Proceedings of the International Conference on Recent Advances in Natural Language Processing (RANLP)*. Borovets, Bulgaria.

Jerry R. Hobbs. 1985. Ontological promiscuity. In William C. Mann, editor, *Proceedings of the 23rd Annual Meeting of the Association for Computational Linguistics (ACL)*, pages 61–9. The Association for Computational Linguistics. Chicago, Illinois.

Jerry R. Hobbs. 1992. Metaphor and abduction. In A. Ortony, J. Slack, and O. Stock, editors, *Communication from an Artificial Intelligence Perspective: Theoretical and Applied Issues*, pages 35–58. Springer, Berlin, Heidelberg.

Jerry R. Hobbs, Mark Stickel, Douglas Appelt, and Paul Martin. 1993. Interpretation as abduction. *Artificial Intelligence*, 63(1–2):69–142.

Naoya Inoue and Kentaro Inui. 2012. Large-scale cost-based abduction in full-fledged first-order predicate logic with cutting plane inference. In Luis Fariñas del Cerro, Andreas Herzig, and Jérôme Mengin, editors, *Proceedings of the 13th European Conference on Logics in Artificial Intelli-*

gence (*JELIA*), pages 281–93. Springer. Toulouse, France.

George Lakoff. 1992. The contemporary theory of metaphor. In A. Ortony, editor, *Metaphor and Thought*, pages 202–51. Cambridge University Press, Cambridge, UK, second edition.

George Lakoff and Mark Johnson. 1980. *Metaphors We Live By*. University of Chicago Press, Chicago, Illinois.

Linlin Li and Caroline Sporleder. 2010. Using Gaussian mixture models to detect figurative language in context. In Jan Hajic, Sandra Carberry, and Stephen Clark, editors, *Proceedings of the 48th Annual Meeting of the Association for Computational Linguistics* (*ACL*), pages 297–300. The Association for Computational Linguistics. Uppsala, Sweden.

Rutu Mulkar, Jerry R. Hobbs, and Eduard Hovy. 2007. Learning from reading syntactically complex biology texts. In *Proceedings of the AAAI Spring Symposium on Logical Formalizations of Commonsense Reasoning*, pages 132–7. AAAI Press.

Srinivas Narayanan. 1997. *Knowledge-based action representations for metaphor and aspect* (*KARMA*). Ph.D. thesis, University of California, Berkeley.

Srinivas Narayanan. 1999. Moving right along: A computational model of metaphoric reasoning about events. In Jim Hendler and Devika Subramanian, editors, *Proceedings of the 16th National Conference on Artificial Intelligence*, pages 121–7. AAAI Press / The MIT Press. Orlando, Florida.

Joakim Nivre, Johan Hall, and Jens Nilsson. 2006. Maltparser: A data-driven parser-generator for dependency parsing. In *Proceedings of the Fifth International Conference on Language Resources and Evaluation* (*LREC*). European Language Resources Association. Genoa, Italy.

Ekaterina Ovchinnikova, Jerry R. Hobbs, Niloofar Montazeri, Michael C. McCord, Theodore Alexandrov, and Rutu Mulkar-Mehta. 2011. Abductive reasoning with a large knowledge base for discourse processing. In Johan Bos and Stephen Pulman, editors, *Proceedings of the Ninth International Conference on Computational Semantics* (*IWCS*), pages 225–34. The Association for Computational Linguistics.

Ekaterina Ovchinnikova, Ross Israel, Suzanne Wertheim, Vladimir Zaytsev, Niloofar Montazeri, and Jerry Hobbs. 2014. Abductive inference for interpretation of metaphors. In *Proceedings of the Second Workshop on Metaphor in NLP*, pages 33–41. The Association for Computational Linguistics.

Ekaterina Shutova. 2010. Automatic metaphor interpretation as a paraphrasing task. In *Proceedings of Human Language Technologies – North American Chapter of the Association for Computational Linguistics* (*HLT-NAACL*), pages 1029–37. The Association for Computational Linguistics.

Ekaterina Shutova, Lin Sun, and Anna Korhonen. 2010. Metaphor identification using verb and noun clustering. In *Proceedings of the 23rd International Conference on Computational Linguistics* (*COLING*), pages 1002–10. The Association for Computational Linguistics. Beijing, China.

Ekaterina Shutova, Tim Van de Cruys, and Anna Korhonen. 2012. Unsupervised metaphor paraphrasing using a vector space model. In *Proceedings of the 24th International Conference on Computational Linguistics: Posters*, pages 1121–30. Mumbai, India.

Yulia Tsvetkov, Leonid Boytsov, Anatole Gershman, Eric Nyberg, and Chris Dyer. 2014. Metaphor detection with cross-lingual model transfer. In *Proceedings of the 52nd Annual Meeting of the Association for Computational Linguistics* (*Volume 1: Long Papers*), pages 248–58. Association for Computational Linguistics. Baltimore, Maryland.

A Corpus of Rich Metaphor Annotation

Jonathan Gordon[1], **Jerry R. Hobbs**[1], **Jonathan May**[1], **Michael Mohler**[2], **Fabrizio Morbini**[3], **Bryan Rink**[2], **Marc Tomlinson**[2], and **Suzanne Wertheim**[4]
[1] USC Information Sciences Institute, {jgordon, hobbs, jonmay}@isi.edu
[2] Language Computer Corp., {michael, bryan, marc}@languagecomputer.com
[3] USC Institute for Creative Technologies, morbini@ict.usc.edu
[4] Worthwhile Research & Consulting, worthwhileresearch@gmail.com

Abstract

Metaphor is a central phenomenon of language, and thus a central problem for natural language understanding. Previous work on the analysis of metaphors has identified which *target* concepts are being thought of and described in terms of which *source* concepts, but this is not adequate to explain what motivates the use of particular metaphors. This work proposes the use of *conceptual schemas* to represent the underspecified scenarios that motivate a metaphoric mapping. To support the creation of systems that can understand metaphors in this way, we have created and are publicly releasing a corpus of manually validated metaphor annotations.

1 Introduction

Lakoff and Johnson (1980) wrote that "the essence of metaphor is understanding and experiencing one kind of thing in terms of another." Our mental, *conceptual metaphors* (CMs) relate the immediate subject matter of a *target* conceptual domain such as *Argument* to a (usually more concrete) *source* domain such as *War*. These conceptual links are exhibited in speech or text as *linguistic metaphors* (LMs), such as "Your claims are indefensible". Metaphors include both fixed-form expressions, such as "won the argument", and novel expressions, such as "threw a fragmentation grenade at her premise". Natural language systems that are not specially equipped to interpret metaphors will behave poorly on metaphoric text. For instance, a document classifier should distinguish between text about a war and text using war as a metaphor to talk about poverty.

The metaphors people use can also provide insights into their attitudes and preconceptions. Examining metaphors allows us to empirically contrast individual speakers, groups, or entire cultures. Even when an expression is common and might not be consciously metaphoric for the speaker, it can fit a metaphoric structuring of the concept being discussed.

Metaphors are not produced at random. Rather, different metaphoric structurings highlight—and hide—different aspects of the target concept. Furthermore, based on theoretical frameworks developed as part of our research, there seems to be a small set of scenarios, central to human existence, that are called upon metaphorically to make sense of more complex or abstract concepts. These include, e.g., threats to a person's health and safety and mitigators of such such threats.

It is in light of this analysis that we approach the annotation of metaphors for interpretation, explanation, and comparison. While previous work, e.g., Shaikh et al. (2014), has produced collections of linguistic metaphors annotated with source and target concepts, such annotations do not capture the scenarios that inform a metaphoric mapping. For instance, the sentences

> Democracy has crushed our dreams.
> Extremists have crushed our democracy.

are both about the source–target pair ⟨*Physical Harm*, *Democracy*⟩, but with contrasting views: In the first, democracy is seen as a threat, while in the second it is being threatened. In this paper, we present an annotation scheme that draws such distinctions, and

Proceedings of the Third Workshop on Metaphor in NLP, pages 56–66,
Denver, Colorado, June 5, 2015. ©2015 Association for Computational Linguistics

we use it to create a corpus of metaphor annotations, which we are releasing to support the creation of tools for the deeper automated analysis of metaphors.

2 Related Work

All corpora contain metaphors, however even those general corpora that give semantic interpretations, e.g., the AMR corpus (Knight et al., 2014), do not address—or do not consistently address—metaphors. Computational research on metaphor has focused on the problems of (1) identifying linguistic metaphors in text (e.g., Fass, 1991; Birke and Sarkar, 2006; Steen et al., 2010; Shutova et al., 2010; Li and Sporleder, 2010) and then (2) identifying the source and target concepts invoked by each linguistic metaphor (e.g., Narayanan, 1997; Barnden and Lee, 2002; Agerri et al., 2007; Shutova, 2010; Ovchinnikova et al., 2014; Gordon et al., 2015).

The corpora of (varyingly annotated) metaphors that have been released to date are not sufficient to tell the story of why a metaphor was invoked or to allow the meaningful comparison of metaphors used by different individuals or even entire cultures. MetaBank (Martin, 1994) provided sets of cross-domain mappings, organized by a small set of important abstract metaphors, adapted from the Berkeley Metaphor List. The latter was expanded into the Master Metaphor List (Lakoff et al., 1991), which gives a hierarchically organized set of conceptual metaphors (i.e., source–target mappings) and supporting examples of linguistic metaphors. The Italian Metaphor Database (Alonge, 2006), the work of Shutova et al. (2013) annotating the British National Corpus (BNC Consortium, 2001), and the large-scale, multilingual work of Shaikh et al. (2014) and Mohler et al. (2014) all focus on the identification of source and target concepts.

Unlike other work manually or automatically annotating metaphors in text, the focus of this paper is not on whether text is metaphorical or not, or which concept domains the metaphors involve, but on the meaning (or "story") of each metaphor. For instance, from the text

> ...changes over the last couple centuries have increased how much democracy infests our [political] system ...

we can identify the verb "infests" as an instance of the source concept *Parasite* and "democracy" as the target *Democracy*. What is absent from this annotation is why we consider this to be so, and what underlying story gives the metaphorical expression heft, e.g.,

> *Democracy is seen as a parasite because it poses a threat to the health of the political system that it "infests".*

In the following section we describe the annotation we use to produce a corpus that meets this standard.

3 Metaphor Representation

We desire a rich structured markup to represent the meaning of metaphors in terms of the speaker's motivation. For this, we introduce a set of ontological categories with associated schema representations.

This builds on previous work mapping linguistic metaphors to their conceptual source and target domains. The *source domain* of the metaphor is the loose set of related concepts used to metaphorically describe the *target domain*. There are no theoretical or practical limitations on the set of target domains that can be described by metaphors. The set of possible source domains is also unbounded, but people commonly draw upon a small set of familiar scenarios in order to make sense of more abstract or complex experiences.

For this work, we recognize 70 source domains. This list is the result of a three-year bottom-up process, where new metaphors were observed, clustered, and assigned a label. Source domains were split or consolidated to better fit the data. The list is necessarily arbitrary, relying on human judgment of when two source domains are distinct.

While 70 source domains abstract over individual linguistic metaphors, 14 *ontological categories* abstract over the source domains. An ontological category is a collection of one or more scenarios that are conceptually related. The choice of ontological categories was based on extensive data analysis, but, as with the source domains, ultimately relies on human judgment. The category of Health and Safety, for instance, includes metaphors from the source domains *Food*, *Medicine*, *Physical Harm*, and *Protection*, among others. The ontological categories are:

1. Health and Safety
2. Journey

3. Conflict
4. Power and Control
5. Engineering and Business
6. Morality and Justice
7. Systematic Explanations
8. Plants
9. Animals
10. Human Life Cycle and Relations
11. Darkness and Light
12. High and Low
13. Nature
14. Embodied Experience

A scenario in an ontological category is a coherent set of roles. Each scenario can be represented by a *conceptual schema*, the set of properties or components that were deemed essential to represent the roles that elements can play in metaphors about the scenario. Each schema was designed based on the analysis of a variety of metaphors for the scenario. Most categories are sufficiently coherent that they can be described by a single overarching *über schema*, while a few, such as Nature, consist of diverse scenarios and thus require multiple schemas. A scenario is added to a category when it is common and is conceptually distinct from the other scenarios in the category, reflected by a low overlap in schema elements.

Each schema is simplified as much as possible while retaining the ability to capture the basic meaning of the scenario. Additional meaning of the metaphor comes from the specific source and target domains involved, and from the particulars of the sentence and the discourse context. The schema analysis of metaphors cannot capture the full meaning of each linguistic metaphor, but it is a step toward a (notional) complete analysis.

We represent a schema as an unordered set of labeled slots, whose values can be

- null (i.e., the slot is not instantiated);
- a text excerpt from the linguistic metaphor (not altered or rearranged); or
- one of a closed-class set of values defined for that slot.

Then, for each linguistic metaphor in a text, a basic explanation of the metaphor is an instantiation of the schema for an ontological source category. A successful annotation should contain enough information, including the choice of the schema, to allow a natural language generator (human or otherwise) to construct an explanatory sentence.

For a selection of the categories, we now provide the corresponding annotation guidelines.[1] These include a detailed description of the scenarios and the elements that define their schemas. The scenario descriptions also serve to explain the schema slots to end-users, e.g., for comparing metaphors used by different groups.

Each schema slot is accompanied by an illustrative list of *lexical triggers*, which are text constructions that may identify the slot's value. For closed-class slots, the legal values are given in uppercase. Each schema is followed by example metaphor annotations, primarily drawn from the US gun control debate. These analyses include the identification of source and target conceptual domains.

Category: Health and Safety

People want to stay safe and healthy. Some things in the world are *threats* to the health and safety of the *threatened*. Other things are *protection* against these threats or are *beneficial*.

— **Threat**, e.g., monsters, tsunamis, diseases, parasites, "overdose of *x*", "evil *x*".
— **Threatened**, e.g., "sick *x*", "*x* overdoses", "*x* is threatened", "*x* is infested", "*x* is contaminated".
— **Protection** or mitigation of threats, e.g., medicine, protection, shelter, "*x* alleviates".
— **Beneficial** or necessary things, e.g., "*x* is the beating heart of *y*", doctors, "appetite for *x*".

Examples:

> "This is how irrationally fearful are [sic] of guns some people are. Seems any *exposure* to *firearms* is a horrific tragedy. Even teaching gun safety is a travesty."

— **Source**: *Disease*
— **Target**: *Guns*
— **Threat**: "firearms"
— **Threatened**: "some people"

[1] The full set of annotation guidelines is included with the released corpus.

> "Back in the 1760's there was a far greater amount of threat that a *gun* could potentially *alleviate* than there is for a person at a local starbucks [sic]."

— **Source**: *Medicine/Physical Burden*
— **Target**: *Guns*
— **Protection**: "gun"

Category: Journey

An *agent* on a journey wants to reach their *goal*. Some things—*vehicle*s—facilitate movement towards a destination. Other things—*barrier*s—hinder movement towards a destination. Any movement forward or back causes *change* to increase or decrease (*change type*).

— **Agent**: the person on a journey, e.g., "*x* flies", "*x* travels", "*x* marches", "journey of *x*", "progression of *x*".
— **Goal**: the destination of the journey, e.g., destination, escape, summit, "advance toward *x*", "road to *x*", "steps toward *x*", "door to *x*".
— **Vehicle**: the facilitator of the journey, e.g., "straight pathway of *x*", "engine of *x*", "*x* provides access to".
— **Barrier**: a thing that impedes the journey, e.g., "maze of *x*", road block, "obstructive *x*", obstacle, "*x* restrains", "*x* ensnares", labyrinthine.
— **Change**, e.g., "*x* advances", "*x* progresses", "retreat of *x*", "*x* go backwards", "*x* reversed course".
— **Change Type**:
  - INCREASE, e.g., advances, increases, progresses.
  - DECREASE, e.g., retreats, decreases, diminishes.

Examples:

> "...we need to accept the historical account of the second amendment for what it actually is, and move forward *in advancing gun rights* with a full understanding of the historical truth. Only then will gun rights be on a solid foundation."

— **Source**: *Forward Movement*
— **Target**: *Gun Rights*
— **Agent**: "we"
— **Goal**: "gun rights be on a solid foundation"
— **Vehicle**: "accept the historical account of the second amendment for what is actually is"
— **Change**: "gun rights"
— **Change Type**: INCREASE

> "The *retreat* of *gun control* is over."

— **Source**: *Backward Movement*
— **Target**: *Control of Guns*
— **Change**: "gun control"
— **Change Type**: DECREASE

Category: Conflict

There are two opposing *side*s in a conflict, one of which may be the *enemy* of the speaker. The conflict has structure and plays out according to the rules of engagement. A component of the conflict may be an *aid*, which helps progress toward the goal of winning. At the end, one side is a *winner* and the other side is a *loser*. If your side wins, it is success; if it loses, it is failure. The conflict may have different stakes, e.g., losing a war is more serious than losing a football game.

— **Conflict**, e.g., "game of *x*", "battle of *x*", "*x* competition", "*x* debate", "fight in *x*", "the *x* war", "inning of *x*", "struggle of *x*".
— **Side**, e.g., "*x* team", "*x* forces", "compete with *x*", "challenge *x*", "winning against *x*", "rival to *x*", "*x* combats *y*", "*x* scored", "*x* is battling".
— **Enemy** or competitor of the speaker, e.g., "*x* are terrorists", "*x* are evildoers", "opposing *x*", "fighting *x*", "*x* is our enemy".
— **Winner**, e.g., "*x* wins", "*x* victory", "victorious *x*", "*x* conquered", "victory of *x* over..."
— **Loser**, e.g., "*x* loses", "defeated *x*", "surrender of *x*", "defeat of *x*", "*x* capitulates".
— **Aid**, a component of the conflict that helps toward winning, e.g., a home run, "sword of *x*", "brandish *x*", "wield *x*", "*x* is a useful weapon".

Examples:

> "Whether George W. Bush or Al Gore ends up **winning** the *presidency*, the Constitution charts a course for him ..."

— **Source**: *Competition*
— **Target**: *Government*

— **Conflict**: presidency
— **Side**: "George W. Bush"
— **Side**: "Al Gore"

> "We agree that *gun control* will *win* because Americans aren't willing to kill over it."

— **Source**: *Competition / Game*
— **Target**: *Control of Guns*
— **Side**: "Americans"
— **Winner**: "gun control"

Category: Power and Control

A being may have power and control over another being. Levels of control and the autonomy of the subservient person vary. There is resentment and anger when autonomy levels are perceived as too low.

There are two distinct—but related—scenarios in Power and Control, which are annotated differently:

Scenario: Power and Control: God

A *god* is a sacred being that a *worshipper* considers to rightly have power over humans due to its innate superiority, including its holiness, wisdom, or might. The *legitimacy* of a non-divine being that has been elevated and worshipped as a god is false; otherwise, it is true.

— **God**, e.g., "*x* cult", "idolize *x*", "sacred *x*", "worship of *x*", "temple of *x*", "divine *x*", "*x* idol", "holy *x*".
— **Worshipper**, e.g., "*x* idolizes", "*x* praises", "*x* worships".
— **Legitimacy**:
  - TRUE, e.g., divine, sacred.
  - FALSE, e.g., cult, false god, idol.

Examples:

> "On the other hand when *guns* become *idols* we can document how their presence transforms the personalities of individuals and entire communities."

— **Source**: *A God*
— **Target**: *Guns*
— **God**: "guns"
— **Legit**: FALSE

> "Thus, independence of the *Judiciary* is *enshrined* in the Constitution for the first time, which is rightly considered a historic landmark."

— **Source**: *A God*
— **Target**: *Government*
— **God**: "independence of the Judiciary"
— **Legit**: TRUE

Scenario: Power and Control: Human

Sometimes there is a clearly marked hierarchy among people, where a *servant* serves the will of a *leader*. The *degree* of oppression or submission may be low, in which case the servant is more thoroughly controlled, like a slave. Higher degrees of oppression are generally seen more negatively.

— **Leader**: who or what has power, e.g., "*x* ordered", "assisted *x*", "served *x*", "*x* enslaves", "*x* oppression", "*x* reigns", "*x* is king".
— **Servant**: who or what is assisting or being controlled, e.g., "*x* assisted", "*x* served", "enslaves *x*", "*x* obeys", "servile *x*", "*x* works for".
— **Degree**:
  - HIGH: like a slave, e.g., slave, slave driver, dominance.
  - LOW: like a servant, e.g., served, assisted, helped.

Examples:

> "Instead we watch *gun control command* the media filling every mind in the world with its hatred and fear of guns."

— **Source**: *Leader*
— **Target**: *Control of Guns*
— **Leader**: "gun control"
— **Servant**: "the media"
— **Degree**: HIGH

> "Guns prevent crime, *guns assist* crime, guns cause accidental deaths, guns turn minor disagreement into a [sic] deadly encounters."

— **Source**: *Servant*
— **Target**: *Guns*
— **Leader**: "crime"
— **Servant**: "guns"
— **Degree**: LOW

4 Metaphor Annotation

While annotated datasets are needed for computational work on metaphor, creating them is a difficult problem. Generating any rich semantic annotation from scratch is a daunting task, which calls for an annotation standard with a potential for high inter-annotator agreement (IAA). Even trained annotators using specialized tools will frequently disagree on the meaning of sentences—see, e.g., Banarescu et al. (2013). Previous work has found it challenging even to manually annotate metaphors with source and target domain labels (Shutova et al., 2013).

Part of the difficulty is a lack of consensus about annotation schemes. The specification given above is particular to the features that motivate metaphor production and thus allow us to readily explain the meanings of metaphors. It is worth considering the relation of this metaphor-specific annotation to general semantic representation. A significant amount of work has gone into the creation of semantically annotated corpora such as the 13,000-sentence AMR 1.0 (Knight et al., 2014) or the 170,000 sentences annotated in FrameNet (Fillmore et al., 2003). This kind of sentential semantic representation captures the literal meaning of metaphoric sentences. Combined with an LM identification system, such semantic analyses could provide a basis for automatic metaphor interpretation. However, this interpretation would still need to be within a framework for metaphoric meaning, like the one outlined above.

4.1 LM Discovery

This work does not begin with a standard corpus and annotate it. Rather, we rely on the work of Mohler et al. (2015) to manually and automatically gather a diverse set of metaphors from varied text. These metaphors pertain to target concepts in the areas of governance (e.g., *Democracy*, *Elections*), economic inequality (e.g., *Taxation*, *Wealth*), and the US debate on gun control (e.g., *Gun Rights*, *Control of Guns*). Some metaphors were identified manually, using web searches targeted at finding examples or particular source–target pairs. More potential metaphors were found automatically in text by a variety of techniques, described in that work, and were partly verified by human annotators in an ad hoc active learning setting.

The sentences are intentionally varied in the viewpoints of the authors as well as the genres of writing, which include press releases, news articles, weblog posts, online forum discussions, and social media. There are trade-offs in the use of this data set versus the annotation of metaphors in a general-purpose corpus: We will necessarily miss some kinds of metaphors that we would find if we annotated each sentence in a corpus, but this also lets us find more interesting and unique metaphors about a small set of target concepts than we would in that approach. That is, our choice of sentences exhibits the diversity of ways that people can conceptualize the same set of target concepts.

4.2 Manual Annotation and Active Expansion

The corpus of annotated metaphoric sentences are all manually validated. Some of these were annotated entirely manually: An initial set of 218 metaphors were annotated by two of the authors, including three to five examples instantiating each schema slot for the most common schemas. Along with these annotations, we identified potential lexical triggers for each slot, like the examples given in section 3.

A prototype classifier was created and was trained on these annotations. It suggested possible annotations, which were then manually verified or corrected. The use of an automatic classifier is important as it (1) allowed for the more rapid creation of a human-verified dataset and (2) suggests the suitability of these annotations for the creation of future tools for automated metaphor analysis.

The prototype classifier used an instance-based classification approach. Each scenario and schema slot were represented by one to three example linguistic metaphors. The example metaphors were then automatically expanded based on four key features:

1. *The source concept used in the linguistic metaphor.* Each source concept is associated with one or more schemas and their scenarios. These were identified during the development of the ontological categories and the annotation guidelines. An example of an ambiguous source concept is *Body of Water*. A linguistic metaphor about "an ocean of wealth" would be classified in the Nature category, while threatening water, e.g., "a tsunami of guns", would be classified in Health and Safety.

2. *Grammatical and morphological information in the linguistic metaphor's context.* The sentence containing the linguistic metaphor was annotated with the Malt parser (Nivre et al., 2006), giving the dependency path between the LM's source and target. Custom code collapses the dependency relations across prepositions, integrating the preposition into the relation. The dependency path is used in combination with the lexical item, its voice (if applicable), part of speech, and valence. Expansion is allowed to linguistic metaphors with similar characteristics. For instance, "we were attacked by gun control" (attacked-VERB-passive PREP-BY target, transitive) indicates that the target concept is agentive and should fill a slot that supports agency of the target, such as Threat in Health and Safety or Enemy in the Conflict schema.

3. *The affective quality of the linguistic metaphor.* This feature further disambiguates between potential schema slots, e.g., Threat vs Protection in the Health and Safety schema. The affective quality of the target concept can be used to disambiguate which slot a particular linguistic metaphor should map to.

   We determine the affective quality of the LM by the interaction between the source and target concepts similar to Strzalkowski et al. (2014). This involves two questions: (1) Is the source viewed positively, negatively, or neutrally? (2) How do the target concept, and particularly the features of the target concept that are made salient by the LM, interact with the affective quality of the source concept? This is determined by the use of a set of rules that define the affective quality of the metaphor through the target concept, its semantic relation with the source concept, and the valence of the source concept. E.g., in the linguistic metaphor "cure gun control", we can assign "gun control" to the Threat slot in Health and Safety because "gun control" is seen as negative here.

4. *Semantic representation of the source lexeme.* This is used to identify semantically similar lexical items. The semantic representation is composed of three sub-components:

(a) *Dependency-based distributional vector space.* Each word's vector is derived from its neighbors in a large corpus, with both the dependency relation and the lexical neighbor used to represent dimensions for each vector, e.g., NSUBJ_Cure (Mohler et al., 2014). Prepositions collapsed and added to the dependency relation, e.g., PREP_TO_Moon. The distributional representation space ensures that words are only closely related to words that are semantically and grammatically substitutable. (This is in contrast to document- or sentence-based representations, which do not strictly enforce grammatical substitutability.) We do not apply dimensionality reduction. While dimension reduction assists the representation of low-occurrence words, it also forces words to be represented by their most frequent sense, e.g., "bank" would only be similar to other financial institutions. By using an unreduced space, rarer senses of words are maintained in the distributional space.

(b) *Sense-disambiguation* provides an enhancement of the distributional vector. For lexical seed terms that can map to multiple concepts, we use vector subtraction to remove conceptual generalizations that are made to the wrong "sense" of the lexical item. E.g., the distributional vector for "path" contains a component associated with computational file systems; this component is removed by subtracting the neighbors of "filename" from the neighbors of "path". This type of adjustment is only possible because the vectors exist in a space where the alternative senses have been preserved. This step is currently done manually, using annotators to identify expansions along inappropriate senses.

(c) *Recognition of antonyms.* Antonyms generally have identical selectional preferences (e.g., direct objects of "increase" can also "decrease") and almost identical distributional vectors. While they generally support mapping into the same ontological category, they often imply mapping to opposite slots. E.g., the subjects of both "attack" and "defend" map into the Health and Safety schema, but the former is a Threat and the latter is Protection. We use WordNet (Fellbaum, 1998) to identify antonyms of the lexical seed terms to ensure that generalizations do not occur to antonymous concepts.

Novel linguistic metaphors fitting these expansions are classified into that particular scenario and slot.

Two issues arose related to coverage: The first is with the lack of coverage for mapping linguistic metaphors into schemas due to the low recall of systems that link non-verbal predicates and their semantic arguments. Metaphors occur across a variety of parts of speech, so extending argument detection to non-verbal predicates is an area for future work. The second issue involves insufficient recall of slot values. The schemas allow for a rich population of role and property values. While some of these are metaphorical, many also occur as literal arguments to a predicate. They can also occur in the same sentence or in neighboring sentences.

4.3 Validation

This system gave us a noisy stream of classifications based on our initial seed set. For two iterations of the system's output, three of the authors were able to quickly mark members of this data stream as correct or not. For the second round of output validation, three of the authors also identified the correct schema slot for erroneous classifications. These iterations could be repeated further for greater accuracy and coverage, providing an ever better source of annotations for rapid human validation. For the first round of validation, we used a binary classification: correct (1) or incorrect (0). For the second round of validation, system output was marked as completely right (1), not perfect (0), or completely wrong (-1). The counts for these validations are shown in Table 1.

Fewer of the annotations in the second round were marked as correct, but this reflects the greater variety of schema slots being distinguished in those annotations than were included in the initial output. One limitation on the accuracy of the classifier for both rounds is that it was not designed to specially handle closed-class slots. As such, the text-excerpt values output for these slots were rejected or were manually corrected.

To measure inter-annotator agreement, 200 of the schema instantiations found by the system were doubly verified. (The extra annotations are not included in Table 1.) For those from Round 2, we collapse the trinary rating to the original binary classification. The pairwise Cohen κ scores reflect good agreement in spite of the difficulty of the task:

Annotators	Cohen κ
1 and 2	0.65
1 and 3	0.42

Rating	Round 1		Round 2	
1	515	67%	732	41%
0	253	33%	752	43%
-1			283	16%

Table 1: Ratings for two rounds of validation of automatic annotations. Correct = 1, incorrect = 0. For round two, ratings for incorrect annotations are split into 0 (not perfect) and -1 (completely wrong).

4.4 Corpus Analysis

The resulting corpus is a combination of entirely manual annotations, automatic annotations that have been manually verified, and automatic annotations that have been manually corrected. The annotation and verification process is guided by the definitions of the scenarios and their schemas, as given in section 3. However, it also relies on the judgment of the individual annotators, who are native English speakers trained in linguistics or natural language processing. The creation of the corpus relies on our intuitions about what is a good metaphor and what are the likely meaning and motivation of each metaphor.

The result of these initial annotations and the manual validation and correction of the system output was a corpus containing 1,771 instantiations of metaphor schema slots, covering all 14 of the schemas, with more examples for schemas such as Health and Safety and Journey that occur more frequently in text. Statistics on the extent and distribution of annotations for the initial release of the corpus are given in Table 2.

The corpus is being publicly released and is available at ⟨http://purl.org/net/metaphor-corpus⟩.

5 Summary

Metaphors play an important role in our cognition and our communication, and the interpretation of metaphor is essential for natural language processing. The computational analysis of metaphors requires

Category	Scenarios	Sentences	Slots	Slot–Value Pairs	Sources	Targets
1. Health & Safety	1	416	4	429	30	11
2. Journey	1	116	6	132	28	11
3. Conflict	1	407	6	482	18	12
4. Power & Control	2	102	6	125	11	12
5. Engineering & Business	3	206	10	219	24	12
6. Morality & Justice	1	129	8	146	9	11
7. Systematic Explanations	1	15	5	19	4	5
8. Plants	1	10	3	12	2	5
9. Animals	1	11	2	11	2	3
10. Human Life Cycle...	1	16	4	32	4	5
11. Darkness & Light	1	9	3	16	2	5
12. High & Low	1	45	5	68	9	10
13. Nature	3	25	8	37	7	6
14. Embodied Experience	3	21	11	42	4	8
Total	20	1450	81	1770	68	12

Table 2: Statistics for the corpus of annotations being released. Each category consists of one or more scenarios. For a variety of sentences, the corpus gives instantiations (slot–value pairs) of the slots in the schema for each scenario. Each linguistic metaphor is also tagged as being about one or more source and target concepts. All counts are for unique entries, except for slot–value pairs, which includes duplicates when they occur in the data. Some sentences contain more than one metaphor, so the number of unique sentences is less than the sum of unique sentences for each schema.

the availability of data annotated in such a way as to support understanding. The ontological source categories described in this work provide a more insightful view of metaphors than the identification of source and target concepts alone. The instantiation of the associated conceptual schemas can reveal how a person or group conceives of a target concept—e.g, is it a threat, a force of oppression, or a hindrance to a journey? The schema analysis cannot capture the full meaning of metaphors, but it distills their essential viewpoints. While some types of metaphor seem resistant to this kind of annotation, they seem to be in the minority. We have annotated a diverse set of metaphors, which we are releasing publicly. This data is an important step toward the creation of automatic tools for the large-scale analysis of metaphors in a rich, meaningful way.

Acknowledgments

This work was supported by the Intelligence Advanced Research Projects Activity (IARPA) via Department of Defense US Army Research Laboratory contract number W911NF-12-C-0025. The US Government is authorized to reproduce and distribute reprints for Governmental purposes notwithstanding any copyright annotation thereon. Disclaimer: The views and conclusions contained herein are those of the authors and should not be interpreted as necessarily representing the official policies or endorsements, either expressed or implied, of IARPA, DoD/ARL, or the US Government.

References

Rodrigo Agerri, John Barnden, Mark Lee, and Alan Wallington. 2007. Metaphor, inference and domain independent mappings. In Ruslan Mitkov, editor, *Proceedings of the International Conference on Recent Advances in Natural Language Processing (RANLP)*, pages 17–23. Borovets, Bulgaria.

Antonietta Alonge. 2006. The Italian Metaphor Database. In *Proceedings of the Fifth International Conference on Language Resources and Evaluation (LREC)*. European Language Resources Association, Genoa, Italy.

Laura Banarescu, Claire Bonial, Shu Cai, Madalina Georgescu, Kira Griffitt, Ulf Hermjakob, Kevin

Knight, Philipp Koehn, Martha Palmer, and Nathan Schneider. 2013. Abstract meaning representation for sembanking. In *Proceedings of the Linguistic Annotation Workshop*, pages 178–86. The Association for Computational Linguistics.

John A. Barnden and Mark G. Lee. 2002. An artificial intelligence approach to metaphor understanding. *Theoria et Historia Scientiarum*, 6(1):399–412.

Julia Birke and Anoop Sarkar. 2006. A clustering approach for nearly unsupervised recognition of nonliteral language. In Diana McCarthy and Shuly Wintner, editors, *Proceedings of the 11th Conference of the European Chapter of the Association for Computational Linguistics (EACL)*, pages 329–36. The Association for Computational Linguistics, Trento, Italy.

BNC Consortium. 2001. The British National Corpus, v. 2. Distributed by Oxford University Computing Services. URL www.natcorp.ox.ac.uk.

Dan Fass. 1991. met*: A method for discriminating metonymy and metaphor by computer. *Computational Linguistics*, 17(1):49–90.

Christiane Fellbaum, editor. 1998. *WordNet: An Electronic Lexical Database*. MIT Press.

Charles J. Fillmore, Christopher R. Johnson, and Miriam R. L. Petruck. 2003. Background to FrameNet. *International Journal of Lexicography*, 16:235–50.

Jonathan Gordon, Jerry R. Hobbs, and Jonathan May. 2015. High-precision abductive mapping of multilingual metaphors. In *Proceedings of the Third Workshop on Metaphor in NLP*.

Kevin Knight, Lauren Baranescu, Claire Bonial, Madalina Georgescu, Kira Griffitt, Ulf Hermjakob, Daniel Marcu, Martha Palmer, and Nathan Schneifer. 2014. Abstract meaning representation (AMR) annotation release 1.0. Web download.

George Lakoff, Jane Espenson, and Alan Schwartz. 1991. The master metaphor list. Technical report, University of California, Berkeley.

George Lakoff and Mark Johnson. 1980. *Metaphors We Live By*. University of Chicago Press, Chicago, Illinois.

Linlin Li and Caroline Sporleder. 2010. Using Gaussian mixture models to detect figurative language in context. In Jan Hajic, Sandra Carberry, and Stephen Clark, editors, *Proceedings of the 48th Annual Meeting of the Association for Computational Linguistics (ACL)*, pages 297–300. The Association for Computational Linguistics, Uppsala, Sweden.

James H. Martin. 1994. MetaBank: A knowledge-base of metaphoric language conventions. *Computational Intelligence*, 10:134–49.

Michael Mohler, Bryan Rink, David Bracewell, and Marc Tomlinson. 2014. A novel distributional approach to multilingual conceptual metaphor recognition. In *Proceedings of the 25th International Conference on Computational Linguistics (COLING)*. Dublin, Ireland.

Michael Mohler, Marc Tomlinson, and Bryan Rink. 2015. Cross-lingual semantic generalization for the detection of metaphor. In *Computational Linguistics and Intelligent Text Processing*. Springer.

Srinivas Narayanan. 1997. *Knowledge-based action representations for metaphor and aspect (KARMA)*. Ph.D. thesis, University of California, Berkeley.

Joakim Nivre, Johan Hall, and Jens Nilsson. 2006. Maltparser: A data-driven parser-generator for dependency parsing. In *Proceedings of the Fifth International Conference on Language Resources and Evaluation (LREC)*. European Language Resources Association. Genoa, Italy.

Ekaterina Ovchinnikova, Ross Israel, Suzanne Wertheim, Vladimir Zaytsev, Niloofar Montazeri, and Jerry Hobbs. 2014. Abductive inference for interpretation of metaphors. In *Proceedings of the Second Workshop on Metaphor in NLP*, pages 33–41. Association for Computational Linguistics.

Samira Shaikh, Tomek Strzalkowski, Ting Liu, George Aaron Broadwell, Boris Yamrom, Sarah Taylor, Laurie Feldman, Kit Cho, Umit Boz, Ignacio Cases, Yuliya Peshkova, and Ching-Sheng Lin. 2014. A multi-cultural repository of automatically discovered linguistic and conceptual metaphors. In *Proceedings of the International Conference on Language Resources and Evaluation (LREC)*. European Language Resources Association.

Ekaterina Shutova. 2010. Automatic metaphor interpretation as a paraphrasing task. In *Proceedings of Human Language Technologies – North American Chapter of the Association for Computational Linguistics (HLT-NAACL)*, pages 1029–37. The Association for Computational Linguistics.

Ekaterina Shutova, Barry J. Devereux, and Anna Korhonen. 2013. Conceptual metaphor theory meets the data: A corpus-based human annotation study. *Language Resources & Evaluation*, 7(4):1261–84.

Ekaterina Shutova, Lin Sun, and Anna Korhonen. 2010. Metaphor identification using verb and noun clustering. In *Proceedings of the 23rd International Conference on Computational Linguistics (COLING)*, pages 1002–10. The Association for Computational Linguistics, Beijing, China.

Gerald J. Steen, Aletta G. Dorst, J. Berenike Herrman, Anna Kaal, Tina Krennmayr, and Trijntje Pasma. 2010. *A Method for Linguistic Metaphor Identification: From MIP to MIPVU.* John Benjamins, Amsterdam/Philadelphia.

Tomek Strzalkowski, Samira Shaikh, Kit Cho, George Aaron Broadwell, Laurie Feldman, Sarah Taylor, Boris Yamrom, Ting Liu, Ignacio Cases, Yuliya Peshkova, and Elliot Kyle. 2014. Computing affect in metaphors. In *Proceedings of the Second Workshop on Metaphor in NLP*, pages 42–51. Association for Computational Linguistics. Baltimore, MD.

Understanding Cultural Conflicts using Metaphors and Sociolinguistic Measures of Influence

Samira Shaikh[1], Tomek Strzalkowski[1], Sarah Taylor[2], Ting Liu[1], John Lien[1], George Aaron Broadwell[1], Laurie Feldman[1], Boris Yamrom[1], Kit Cho[1] and Yuliya Peshkova[1]

[1]State University of New York – University at Albany [2]Sarah Taylor Consulting LLC
samirashaikh@gmail.com, tomek@albany.edu

Abstract

In this article, we outline a novel approach to the automated analysis of cross-cultural conflicts through the discovery and classification of the metaphors used by the protagonist parties involved in the conflict. We demonstrate the feasibility of this approach on a prototypical conflict surrounding the appropriate management and oversight of gun-ownership in the United States. In addition, we present a way of incorporating sociolinguistic measures of influence in discourse to draw further insights from complex data. The results presented in this article should be considered as illustrative of the types of analyses that can be obtained using our methodology; however, no attempt was made to rigorously validate the specific findings reported here. We address open issues such as how our approach could be generalized to analyze cross cultural conflicts around the world.

1 Introduction

All discourse is a means to convey ideas, fulfill goals and possibly attempt to persuade the listener (Perloff, 2014). Metaphors, which are mapping systems that allow the semantics of a familiar Source domain to be applied to a Target domain so that new frameworks of reasoning can emerge in the Target domain, are pervasive in discourse. Metaphorically rich language is considered highly influential. Persuasion and influence literature (Soppory and Dillard, 2002) indicates messages containing metaphorical language produce somewhat greater attitude change than messages that do not. Metaphors embody a number of elements of persuasive language, including concreteness and imageability (Strzalkowski et al., 2013, Broadwell et al., 2013, Charteris-Black, 2005). Using this line of investigation, we aim to understand the motivations of a group or of a political faction through their discourse, as part of the answer to such questions as: What are the key differences in protagonists' positions? How extensive is a protagonists' influence? Who dominates the discourse? Where is the core of the groups' support?

Our goal is to provide a basis for the analysis of cross-cultural conflicts by viewing the conflict as an ongoing debate or a "dialogue" between protagonists or participants.

In this interpretation, each major protagonist position becomes a "speaker" and the articles, postings, and commentaries published by media outlets representing that position become "utterances" in a debate. The targets (i.e. main concepts) of the conflict are those concepts that align with the main topics (we shall call them meso-topics) of the debate. Protagonists' positions in the conflict are derived from their language use when talking about these meso-topics, particularly the metaphorical language. The relationships between the protagonist positions are determined based on sociolinguistic features of their "utterances", particularly topic control, disagreement, argument diversity, and topical positioning. These and other features allow us to isolate "subgroups" or factions of like-minded individuals, including those that are more extreme (farther apart) and those that are moderate (closer to a "center"). In addition, we look for indicators of influence these groups exert upon each other as well as upon their other audiences (broader public, lawmakers, policy makers, etc.) We thus aim to bring together two emerging technologies to bear upon conflict case analysis: automated metaphor extraction, and automated analysis of the sociocultural aspects of language.

Proceedings of the Third Workshop on Metaphor in NLP, pages 67–76,
Denver, Colorado, June 5, 2015. ©2015 Association for Computational Linguistics

Understanding conflicts in this manner may allow policy-makers facilitate negotiations and discussions across different communities and help bridge contrasting viewpoints and cultural values.

2 Relevant Research

The underlying core of our research is automated, large-scale metaphor extraction. Computational approaches to metaphor to date have yielded only limited scale, often hand-designed systems (Wilks, 1975; Fass, 1991; Carbonell, 1980; Feldman & Narayan, 2004; Shutova & Teufel, 2010; inter alia). Baumer et al. (2010) used semantic role labels and typed dependency parsing in an attempt towards computational metaphor identification. Shutova (2010) employ an unsupervised method of metaphor identification using nouns and verb clustering to automatically impute metaphoricity in a large corpus using an annotated training corpus of metaphors as seeds. Several other similar approaches were reported at the Meta4NLP workshop, e.g., (Mohler et al., 2013; Wilks et al., 2013; Hovy et al., 2013). Strzalkowski et al. (2013) developed a data-driven approach towards the automated extraction of metaphors from text and our approach builds upon their work. The use of metaphor, along with sociocultural aspects of language to understand cross-cultural conflict is novel to our approach. Recent research in computational sociolinguistic has developed methods for automatic assessment of leadership, influence and power in conversation (Broadwell et al., 2012; Shaikh et al., 2012; Strzalkowski et al., 2010) and we draw largely upon this work. Other relevant work includes Nguyen et al. (2013), who look at nonparametric topic modeling as a measure of influence; and Bracewell et al. (2012), who look at a category of social acts to determine measures of leadership; among others. Analysis of positions held by discourse participants has been studied in the realm of political science and computational sociolinguistics (Laver, Benoit & Garry, 2003; Slapin & Proksch, 2008; Lin et al., 2013; Pang & Lee, 2008) and our approach draws parallels from such prior work. Our topical positioning approach is a departure from existing approaches to sentiment analysis (Wiebe, Wilson and Cardie, 2005; Strapparava and Mihalcea, 2008) in looking at a larger context of discourse rather than individual utterances.

3 The Conflict – U.S. Gun Debate

The main hypothesis, and an open research question, is then: can this new technology be effectively applied to understanding of a broad cultural conflict such as may arise in any society where potentially divisive issues exist? To answer this question, we decided to conduct a feasibility study in order to scope out the problem. What we present below is the outcome of this study and possibilities it opened for future research. The actual results of conflict case analysis obtained here are for illustrative purposes only.

To start, we selected a conflict case that is both familiar and has abundance of data available that is easily accessible. The case can be considered as representative both in terms of its overall structure (opposing views, radical and moderate positions, ongoing tension) as well as the debate surrounding it (complexity of language, indirectness, talking about self and the others, etc.). At the same time, its familiarity provided means for immediate assessment of feasibility of the proposed approach: if our subject matter experts could verify the outcome as correct or at least reasonable, it would serve as a point of departure for more rigorous analysis and evaluation of other conflict cases elsewhere in the world.

The cross-cultural conflict we use as an example can be summarized as: "*People disagree about the oversight of guns in the U.S. Some believe that guns and gun safety are the responsibility of individuals; others believe that the Federal Government should manage guns and gun ownership. This contrast in viewpoints has been a source of tension in the US since the colonial era. Although the debate about guns is often thought to be political, its foundation is actually cultural – the proper balance between the rights of the individual citizen and the interests and needs of the majority.*"[1]

The protagonists involved in this conflict are those in favor of individual oversight of guns (INDO for short) and those in favor of Federal Government oversight (GOVTO for short). Given a conflict case such as the above, our goal is to develop methods that will understand and analyze the cultural differences that underlie the conflict and can be ascertained through the use of metaphors by protagonists on either side.

[1] An excerpt from the Guns Practice Case description.

4 Our Approach

4.1 Data Identification and Collection

Our objective was to identify the metaphors that are used to characterize the Gun Case conflict in the U.S. For extracted metaphors to be useful to an analyst in this or any other conflict case, the metaphors must be assigned to a particular protagonist or viewpoint or "side" of whatever debate or conflict is being explored. Without linkage to a viewpoint, discovered metaphors are not particularly illuminating. When dealing with an unfamiliar culture, an analyst may not be able make such a link. Consequently, the system must provide the link. It is the known position, taken by the spokesperson using the metaphor that provides the connection between metaphor and position or side. A spokesperson can be a particular named person – such as the head of an organization espousing the position (i.e., head of the NRA) – but in fact is more commonly a website maintained by an organization for the purposes of promulgating its views.

The first step is the identification of spokespersons and spokesperson sites on all sides of the opinion spectrum. Websites are more helpful than named people, because they provide a large volume of text that is readily accessible in locations that contain high concentrations of material on the focus topic. This step typically requires input from a cultural/political expert; however, it may be approximated (or pre-structured) using the distance calculation based on the Topical Positioning measure (c.f. Section 6).

In the second step, we roughly array these sites along an opinion spectrum, and particularly discover the *extreme positions* at each end of the spectrum, as well as those sites that represent more moderate positions, if still recognizably on each side. This step also requires input by the cultural/political expert; but it may be approximated by the Topical Positioning computation as in first step above, in cases where cultural expertise cannot be obtained.

Once the websites and their positions on opinion spectrum are determined, the third step is collection of data from sites taking a relatively pure and extreme position at each end of the spectrum, after sites have been checked for any access restrictions. Data collection here means downloading snippets of text – passages of up to five sentences – that contain certain terms of relevance to the conflict case under investigation. We start with a broad list of terms that may include potential metaphorical targets as well as other relevant terms. Table 1 shows a subset of these terms in the first column for the Gun Case. Other terms (see Figure 1) are folded under these broad categories in Table 1.

The effect of this collection method is that all automatically extracted metaphors can be automatically tagged as representing one extreme position or the other, based on the initial classification of the site by the cultural expert. These are considered to be core metaphors. This material should be reasonably balanced as to numbers of sites on each side. We make an effort to compensate significantly unbalanced dataset with additional collection on underrepresented side.

Step four is data collection from the sites closer to the middle of the opinion spectrum identified in the second step. When this data is processed for metaphors, they are labeled accordingly as "moderate". We note that "moderate" positions in multi-side conflicts may have different interpretations than in a largely binary conflict of Gun Case. In Table 1, the column Total Passages represents the sum total of passages processed from the extreme and moderate websites.

Target	Total Passages
Gun control	23596
Gun violence	8464
Gun right(s)	9472
Gun law	11150
Gun safety	129
2nd Amendment	516
Gun ownership	1147
Gun owners	2359
Total	57841

Table 1. Distribution of collected data across targets in Gun Case debate

For the Gun Case analysis, two rounds of data collection were conducted. The first round was focused on extreme sites on both sides: data were derived from 10 extreme INDO sites and 20 extreme GOVTO. The greater number of sites in favor of more government oversight was necessary because of the lesser volume of text found in these sites on the average. In the second round of data collection, we added sites that represented moderate positions. Ultimately, we collected data from 45 online sites and collected more than 57,000 text passages as seen in Table 1.

4.2 Identifying Meso-Topics and Targets for Metaphor Extraction

The downloaded data is then processed for meso-topics (frequently mentioned and polarized topics) and metaphors.

The process of identifying the key meso-topics (i.e., the main aspects of the conflict case) has been fully automated in the following 3 steps:

1. Locating frequently occurring topics in text: The initial candidates are noun phrases, proper names (of locations, organizations, positions, events, and other phenomena, but less so of specific individuals). These are augmented with co-referential lexical items: pronouns, variants, and synonyms. The process of selection is quite robust but requires some rudimentary processing capability in the target language: part-of-speech tagging, basic anaphor resolution, and a lexicon/thesaurus.

2. Down selecting the frequent topics to a set of 20-30 meso-topics. The two key criteria for selection are length and polarization. Topic "length" is measured by the number of references to it (either direct or indirect) that form "chains" across the "utterances" that are part of the conflict debate. Topic polarization is measured by the proportion of polarized references to a meso-topic, either positive or negative. For example, the terms gun rights and gun safety are both frequently used and polarized in the Gun Case. In order to keep the analysis manageable, we retain only top 20 to 30 meso-topics, based on their chain lengths.

3. Selecting metaphorical targets and assigning them to case aspects. While all meso-topics are important to the case, only some of them will be targets of metaphors. We determine this by probing metaphor extraction for each of the meso-topics and then eliminating those meso-topics that bring back too few metaphors. In the Gun Case, we used 2% cut-off threshold for productive targets (a typical metaphor to literal ratio is approx. 8%).

Figure 1 shows the meso-topics selected for the Gun Case, and the metaphorical targets identified among them (bold face). Targets are grouped by semantic similarity and assigned to case "aspects".

- Meso-topics identified (mini-ontology)
  - *GUNS:*
    - **guns**, gun, **handguns**, assault weapons, weapons, **firearms**
  - *CONTROL OF GUNS:*
    - **gun control**, **gun law**, gun sales, gun shows, gun safety, (buy guns)
  - *GUN RIGHTS:*
    - **gun rights**, **Second Amendment**, **2nd Amendment**, gun owners, concealed carry, open carry, (bear arms)
  - *GUN VIOLENCE:*
    - **gun violence**, homicide
  - *GUNS FOR PROTECTION:*
    - self-protection
- Targets we use are highlighted

Figure 1. Meso-topics and metaphorical targets identified for the Gun Case

4.3 Extracting Linguistic Metaphors and Building Conceptual Metaphors

Our metaphor extraction system was run over approximately 57 thousand passages collected from the Gun Case protagonists' media outlets, resulting in more than 4000 distinct linguistic metaphors (LMs). These LMs yielded 45 conceptual metaphors (CMs), with 28 CMs on the individual oversight (INDO) side and 17 CMs at the government oversight (GOVTO) side. This uneven split represents the overall data distribution between INDO and GOVTO, reflecting their relative contributions to the Gun Case debate: approximately 70% of contributions (measured in published "utterances") are attributed to the INDO side.

We define the terms LM and CM here: a linguistic metaphor (LM) is an instance of metaphor found in text, for example – "*The roots of gun control are partially about racism*". Here the target is *gun control* and the metaphorical relation is "*roots of*". A prototype source domain for this metaphor could be PLANT, where *gun control* is likened to having properties of a PLANT by the relation *roots of*. A set of linguistic metaphors all pointing to the same source domain, such as PLANT in the above example, would form a conceptual metaphor (CM). The focus of this article is on the use of metaphors towards analyzing a real world conflict scenario. Metaphor extraction is carried out in a data-driven, automated method by our system by using corpus statistics, imageablity and identification of source domains using word vectors to represent source domains. Our work is built upon existing approaches to automated metaphor extraction and source domain mapping (Strzalkowski et al., 2013; Broadwell et al., 2013; Shaikh et al., 2014). Our system extracts linguistic metaphors from text and

Target	INDIVIDUAL OVERSIGHT: Selected CMs/ Total CMs: 28
GUN RIGHTS	ANIMAL (shoot, survive, endanger) BARRIER (push, circumvent, wedge) WAR (battle, victory, jihad) GAME (win, game, champion) A_RIGHT (preserve, lose, violate) CLOTHING (wear, strip, cling) BUILDING (restore, prospect, platform) BUSINESS (sell, expand)
CONTROL OF GUNS	MACHINE (failure of, misfire, defuse) ANIMAL (kill, shoot, evolve) BARRIER (break, ram, hinder) NATURAL_PHYSICAL_FORCE (strong, defy, sweep) WAR (fight, attack, battle) HUMAN_BODY (weak, relax, thrust) BUSINESS (launch, promote) GAME (champion, bandwagon, loser) CLOTHING (tighten, loosen)
GUN VIOLENCE	DISEASE (epidemic, scourge, plague) CRIME (victim, rampant) ACCIDENT (die from, horrific, injury) WAR (battle, fight, escalate)

Table 2. Conceptual Metaphors used by protagonists on the INDO side

Target	GOVERNMENT OVERSIGHT; Selected CMs/Total CMs: 17
GUN RIGHTS	WAR (battle, attack, victory) BUILDING (restore, preserve)
CONTROL OF GUNS	BARRIER (push) NATURAL_PHYSICAL_FORCE (strong) WAR (battle, attack, defend) HUMAN_BODY (strong, tough) CLOTHING (tighten, loosen) PROTECTION (violate, protection)
GUN VIOLENCE	DISEASE (epidemic, survivor) CRIME (victim, perpetrator, rampant) ACCIDENT (tragic, die, gruesome) WAR (fight, carnage, threat) NATURAL_PHYSICAL_FORCE (devastating, brunt of)

Table 3. Conceptual Metaphors used by protagonists on the GOVTO side

automatically groups them together to form conceptual metaphors. The source domains that we refer to in this article are a set of 67 categories that are frequently encountered in metaphorical data.

Tables 2 and 3 below show the overall distribution of CMs found on each side of the debate. Selected representative lexical items associated with each CM are shown in parentheses. Similar tables can be drawn for extreme and moderate positions separately in the debate.

We can now automatically label the metaphors across given positions, extreme or moderate, on each side of the debate. The process of labeling the metaphors then leads to analytic insights into the data, which we shall present in the next section.

5 Preliminary Insights using Metaphorical Data

We report three observations based on automated processing of relevant text sources for presence of metaphorical language used by each protagonist. We should stress here that these are only tentative results that serve as indication of the types of analyses that may be achievable. Rigorous validation is required to confirm these findings; however, it was not our objective of this feasibility study.

5.1 Contrasting Narratives: DISEASE vs. WAR

Both sides of the debate use metaphorical language indicative of their stances on the Gun Case issue. These metaphors invoke a variety of source domains from which we can infer their attitudes toward the issue. Among all source domains invoked by each side, two are predominant:

1. DISEASE is invoked in 21% of all metaphors used by GOVTO
2. WAR is invoked in 20% of all metaphors used by INDO

To determine predominant Conceptual Metaphors for each protagonist (21% and 20% referred above), we rank order the Source Domains (SDs) for each side by number of LMs that use each SD. In Table 4, we show the predominant conceptual metaphors used for key targets by each protagonist.

Target	Government oversight (GOVTO; Anti-gun)	Individual oversight (INDO; Pro-gun)
Gun rights	BUILDING (*)	WAR
Control of guns	NAT_PHYSICAL FORCE	WAR BARRIER
Gun violence	CRIME DISEASE	DISEASE

Table 4. The most representative CMs on both sides of the Gun Debate, by key Targets. Font size indicates relative frequency for top CMs for each target.

WAR and DISEASE/CRIME dominate; however, we note also that the majority of metaphors on GOVTO side come in fact from *gun violence* topic, while on the INDO side the majority comes from the *gun rights* topic. Further breakdown of top source domains for the gun debate targets is elaborated as follows: NATURAL PHYSICAL FORCE, DISEASE and CRIME all seem to contribute towards a cohesive narrative on the GOVTO side, which views the gun issue as an uncontrollable, external, negative force. BARRIER and WAR on INDO side may suggest an overarching narrative of active struggle and overcoming of obstacles.

This resolution of narratives for each side in a conflict is a significant key insight that can be derived from gathered data. Recognizing the underlying narrative in a conflict for any given side can provide ways of resolving conflict by facilitating dialogue that can bridge such differences.

5.2 Sociolinguistic indicators: INDO dominates debate

The INDO side contributes approximately 70% of all content in the Gun Case debate. This proportion does not change substantially even after a deliberate oversampling of data from GOVTO websites. The absolute number of metaphors supplied by INDO is substantially greater than the number produced by GOVTO sites. In addition to contributing the most content and the largest number of metaphors (Figure 4), the INDO side dominates the Gun Case debate according to two key sociolinguistic measures (Broadwell et al., 2012):

1. Showing greater Argument Diversity, which correlates with greater influence. Argument diversity is a sociolinguistic measure manifested in metaphor use by: (a) employment of a larger number of source domains in their metaphors; and (b) Employment of more varied metaphors using distinct relations
2. Using action-oriented language, i.e., the relations in metaphors evoke action for change rather than describing the status quo.

To gather evidence for this insight, we explored the sociocultural indicators of influence exhibited by the INDO side. Figure 4 shows the INDO using significantly more metaphors in most domains, except for DISEASE, CRIME, and NAT-PHYS-FORCE, which are parts of the GOVTO core narrative. Figure 5 further shows that INDO uses more varied relations to evoke these domains, even those SDs used predominantly by GOVTO.

Figure 6 illustrates INDO using more action-oriented language in their metaphors. The two pie charts represent the proportion of lexical items used in LMs that are of the "taking action" type (primarily verbs describing events, such as "*attack*") vs. the "passively observe" (primarily nouns and adjectives, such as "*devastating*").

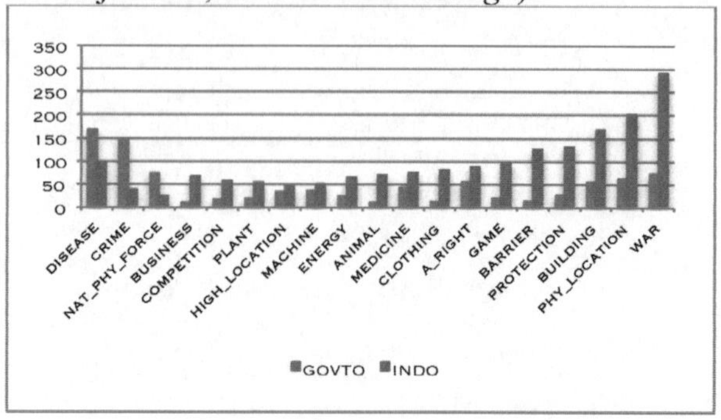

Figure 4. The INDO side (red bars) dominates debate with use of more LMs overall. Here we show those source domains that are used at least 2% of the time overall by both sides and the count of LMs for those Source Domains. Y-axis represents count of metaphors.

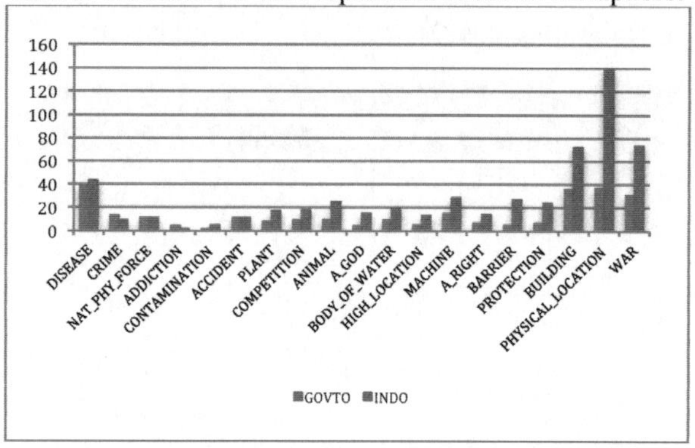

Figure 5. The INDO side dominates debate with richer vocabulary suggesting greater influence. Here we show those source domains that are used at least 2% of the time overall by both sides and the <u>count</u> of distinct relations in the LMs by each protagonist. Y-axis represents count of metaphors.

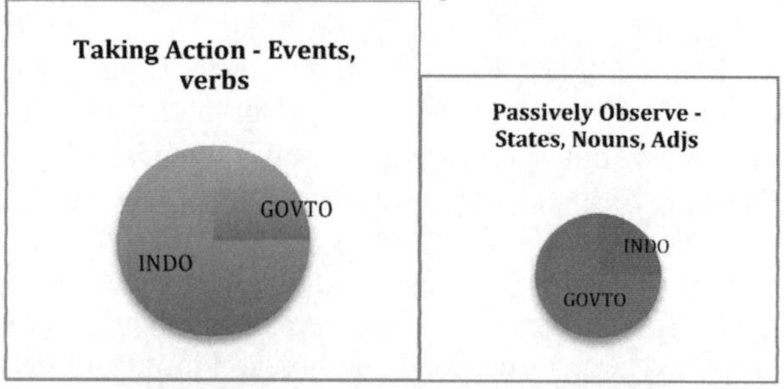

Figure 6. The INDO side dominates debate with use of more action-oriented language. Size of pie chart represents the proportion of metaphors in the source role categories. The "Taking Action" type of metaphors is greater in proportion than "Passively Observe" type of metaphors.

5.3 Topical positioning: INDO occupies the center ground in debate

We wish to calculate the relative positions of protagonists in a debate and to estimate a distance between these positions. We have created a sociolinguistic method of computing those distances using a method called Topical Positioning (Lin et al., 2013). In this section, we shall explain how we arrive at those distances using metaphorical data and give details about the Topical Positioning Method in Section 6.

In order to calculate the positions of extreme and moderate protagonists on each side of the debate, we create a heat-map matrix of metaphor usage for each position. Each matrix represents the numbers of metaphors and Source Domains applied to each key target concept in the debate. Distances between matrices are calculated using cosine measure in multidimensional spaces. Figure 7 shows fragments of heat maps for the extreme GOVTO and INDO positions.

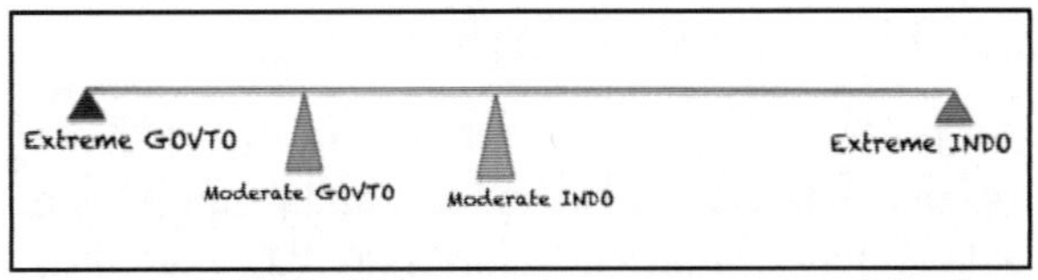

Figure 8. INDO side occupies center ground in the gun debate. We represent each protagonist position on a relative distance "scale"

Using this method, we find that the extreme proponents of the INDO and GOVTO sides are far apart, approximately 0.55 of the maximum theoretical distance of 1.0. Using the same measures, the distance between the INDO moderate position and both INDO and GOVTO extremes is approximately half of the above, or 0.27. This places the INDO moderate position in the center of the spectrum of positions between the two extremes. On the other hand, the language used by the GOVTO moderate position places them closer to the GOVTO extreme. This finding is illustrated in Figure 8.

In this section we presented three observations

GOVTO

	gun control	gun rights	gun laws	second amend.	gun violence
DISEASE	0	0.14	0	0	1.12
CRIME	0.09	0	0	0.13	1.06
N_P_F	0.05	0.91	0.05	0	0.15
BUILDING	0.14	0.06	0.15	0.475	0.104
PHYS_LOCATION	0.2	0.2	0.09	0	0.122
BARRIER	0.26	0.7	0.7	0.11	0.112
WAR	0.09	0.07	0.39	0	0.358

INDO

	gun control	gun rights	gun laws	second amend.	gun violence
DISEASE	0.17	0.103	0.12	0.06	0.71
CRIME	0.46	0	0	0	0.46
N_P_F	0.05	0.05	0.088	0	0
BUILDING	0.12	0.15	0.123	0.27	0
PHYS_LOCATION	0.116	0.108	0.09	0.2	0
BARRIER	0.59	0.7	0.39	0	0
WAR	0.85	0.766	0.42	0.88	0.48

Figure 7. Protagonist matrices shown as heat maps. The intensity of color shows greater proportion of LMs for particular Target-Source mappings. We compute cosine distances between these matrices to determine relative positions of protagonists.

Each $N \times M$ matrix provides the representation of a protagonist position in a debate through their use of metaphors where N represents the number of metaphorical Targets (TCs) in a debate, while M represents the number of source domains (SDs) used in the analysis. Values in each cell represent an average strength score for $TC \rightarrow SD$ mappings found in the data collected from this protagonist media outlets (Shaikh et al., 2014). Empty cells are values below a preset threshold, replaced by 0s. To calculate distances we use a cosine metric; however, other distance measures may also be applicable.

that emerged, from the snapshot of data we collected on this prototypical case and by running automated tools of metaphor and sociolinguistic analyses on the data. These results were confirmed by subject matter experts, who were intimately familiar with the issue. We note that such verification does not constitute a rigorous validation of our findings, the goal of this paper is to present a possible solution and path towards generalizability, validation is a separate issue that we may explore as future work. The selection of a familiar cross-cultural conflict allowed us to propose and test viable solutions that can be adapted to work on previously unknown conflicts.

6 Topical Positioning

While the two sides of the debate use different metaphors to convey their views of the gun issue, it is not immediately clear just how far apart these positions are, and thus how strong or intractable the conflict really is. One possible way to compute the distance between protagonists is to use the method of Topical Positioning (Lin et al., 2013)

In discourse analysis, *Topical Positioning* is defined as the attitude a speaker (our protagonist) has on main topics (meso-topics) of discussion. Speakers in a dialogue, when discussing issues, especially ones with some controversy, will establish their attitude on a topic, classified as for, against, or neutral/undecided.

To establish topical positioning, we first identify meso-topics that are present in a debate, as discussed in Section 4.1. We then distinguish multiple forms in which polarization or valuation is applied to meso-topics in protagonists' utterances such as through express advocacy or disadvocacy or via supporting or dissenting information, and express agreement or disagreement with a polarized statement made in a statement by the same or another protagonist. We create Topical Positioning Vectors representing each protagonist. Table 5 shows a fragment of positional vectors for extreme GOVTO and INDO positions for five meso-topics. In these vectors, value in each cell represents a prevailing combined polarity and intensity towards a meso-topic. We note that meso-topics form a superset of metaphorical targets as explained earlier.

M-topics	Hand guns	firearms	gun owners	gun control	gun rights
INDO	4	5	5	0	5
GOVTO	0	-1	0	5	-1

Table 5. Topical Positioning vectors for extreme GOVTO and INDO positions in the gun debate

Topical Positioning vectors can now be used to calculate distance between protagonists, using standard cosine measure. We used this method to compute 4-ways distances in the Gun Case: between the extreme positions on each side; between the moderate and extreme positions within each side; as well as between moderates and extremes across the sides and compared the distances so obtained to those obtained from metaphorical matrices (Section 5.3). We note that both methods yielded essentially identical results. The distance between extreme positions on INDO and GOVTO side appears to be very large, varying between 0.55 and 0.58. The distances between moderates and between moderates and extremes are appropriately smaller (~0.27). The distance between moderate and extreme INDO places the former in the center between the two extremes. This result is confirmed by the smaller than expected distance between moderate and extreme GOVTO. This may suggest that moderate INDO (thus, the INDO side) dominates the debate by effectively occupying its center.

7 Discussion and Open Issues

In this paper, we presented a preliminary yet innovative approach towards the understanding of cultural conflict through the use of metaphors and sociolinguistic measures of influence. Our approach was illustrated on the analysis on a prototypical case centered on the U.S Gun debate. By casting the problem as an analysis of discourse, or debate between protagonists, we gain significant benefits – we can use established social science methods to draw potentially illuminating and non-trivial insights from otherwise very complex and often conflicted data. We believe that the approach presented here can be generalized to other types of conflict by following the steps detailed in Section 4. It is possible that issues with multiple, clearly distinct sides all aimed at clearly distinguishable solutions to a general issue may need to be dealt with as clusters or will need to be broken down into multiple two- or three-sided conflicts, depending upon the precise goals to be achieved.

Acknowledgments

This paper is based on work supported by the Intelligence Advanced Research Projects Activity (IARPA) via Department of Defense US Army Research Laboratory contract number W911NF-12-C-0024. The U.S. Government is authorized to reproduce and distribute reprints for Governmental purposes notwithstanding any copyright annotation thereon. Disclaimer: The views and conclusions contained herein are those of the authors and should not be interpreted as necessarily representing the official policies or endorsements, either expressed or implied, of IARPA, DoD/ARL, or the U.S. Government.

References

Eric P. S. Baumer, James P. White, and Bill Tomlinson. 2010. Comparing semantic role labeling with typed dependency parsing in computational metaphor identification. In *Proceedings of the NAACL HLT 2010 Second Workshop on Computational Approaches to Linguistic Creativity*, pages 14–22, Los Angeles, California.

David B. Bracewell, and Tomlinson, Marc T. 2012. The Language of Power and its Cultural Influence, In *Proceedings of the 24th International Conference on Computational Linguistics (COLING)*

George Broadwell, Jennifer Stromer-Galley, Tomek Strzalkowski, Samira Shaikh, Sarah Taylor, Umit Boz, Alana Elia, Laura Jiao, Ting Liu and Nick Webb. 2012. *Modeling Socio-Cultural Phenomena in Discourse.* Journal of Natural Language Engineering, Cambridge Press.

George Aaron Broadwell, Umit Boz, Ignacio Cases, Tomek Strzalkowski, Laurie Feldman, Sarah Taylor, Samira Shaikh, Ting Liu, Kit Cho, and Nick Webb. 2013. Using imageability and topic chaining to locate metaphors in linguistic corpora. In *Proceedings of International Conference on Social Computing, Behavioral-Cultural Modeling, & Prediction*, pages 102–109. Washington D.C.

Jaime Carbonell. 1980. Metaphor: A key to extensible semantic analysis. In *Proceedings of the 18th Annual Meeting on Association for Computational Linguistics*.

Jonathan Charteris-Black. 2002. Second language figurative proficiency: A comparative study of Malay and English. *Applied Linguistics* 23(1):104–133.

Dan, Fass. 1991. met*: A Method for Discriminating Metonymy and Metaphor by Computer. *Computational Linguistics*, 17:49-90

Jerome Feldman and Srinivas Narayanan. 2004. Embodied meaning in a neural theory of language. *Brain and Language*, 89(2):385–392.

Dirk Hovy, Shashank Shrivastava, Sujay Kumar Jauhar, Mrinmaya Sachan, Kartik Goyal, Huying Li, Whitney Sanders and Eduard Hovy. 2013. Identifying Metaphorical Word Use with Tree Kernels. In the *Proceedings of the First Workshop on Metaphor in NLP, (NAACL)*. Atlanta.

Michael Laver, Kenneth Benoit, and John Garry. 2003. *Extracting Policy Positions from Political Texts Using Words as Data.* American Political Science Review 97(2): 311–32.

Ching-Sheng Lin, Samira Shaikh, Jennifer Stromer-Galley, Jennifer Crowley, Tomek Strzalkowski and Veena Ravishankar. 2013. Topical Positioning: A New Method for Predicting Opinion Changes in Conversation. In *Proceedings of the Workshop on Language Analysis in Social Media*, June 2013. Atlanta, Georgia. pp 41-48.

Michael Mohler, David Bracewell, David Hinote, and Marc Tomlinson. 2013. Semantic signatures for example-based linguistic metaphor detection. In The *Proceedings of the First Workshop on Metaphor in NLP, (NAACL)*, pages 46–54.

Viet-An Nguyen, Jordan Boyd-Graber, Philip Resnik, Deborah Cai, Jennifer Midberry, and Yuanxin Wang. 2013. *Modeling Topic Control to Detect Influence in Conversations using Nonparametric Topic Models.* Machine Learning, 2013.

Bo Pang & Lillian Lee. 2008. *Foundations and Trends in Information Retrieval* 2, 1–135.

Richard M. Perloff. 2014. *The dynamics of political communication: Media and politics in a digital age.* New York: Routledge.

Samira Shaikh, Tomek Strzalkowski, Jenny Stromer-Galley, Geoge Aaron Broadwell, Sarah Taylor, Ting Liu, Veena Ravishankar, Xiaoai Ren and Umit Boz. 2012. Modeling Influence in Online Multi-Party Discourse. In Proceedings of 2nd International Conference on Social Computing and Its Applications (SCA 2012), Xiangtan, China.Ekaterina Shutova. 2010. Models of metaphors in NLP. In *Proceedings of ACL 2010. Uppsala, Sweden.*

Samira Shaikh, Tomek Strzalkowski, Kit Cho, Ting Liu, George Aaron Broadwell, Laurie Feldman, Sarah Taylor, Boris Yamrom, Ching-Sheng Lin, Ning Sa, Ignacio Cases, Yuliya Peshkova and Kyle Elliot. 2014 . Discovering Conceptual Metaphors using Source Domain Spaces. In *Proceedings of the 4th Workshop on Cognitive Aspects of the Lexicon, pages 210–220, Dublin, Ireland, August 23, 2014.*

Ekaterina Shutova and Simone Teufel. 2010. Metaphor corpus annotated for source - target domain mappings. *In Proceedings of Language Resources and Evaluation Conference 2010*. Malta.

Jonathan B. Slapin and Sven-Oliver Proksch. 2008. "A Scaling Model for Estimating Time-Series Party Positions from Texts" American Journal of Political Science 52(3): 705-722.

Pradeep Sopory, P. and James Price Dillard. 2002. *The Persuasive Effects of Metaphor: A Meta-Analysis.* Human Communication Research, 28: 382–419. doi: 10.1111/j.1468-2958.2002.tb00813.x

Carlo Strapparava, C., and Rada Mihalcea. 2008. Learning to Identify Emotions in Text. In Proceedings of the ACM Conference on Applied Computing ACM-SAC.

Tomek Strzalkowski, George Aaron Broadwell, Jennifer Stromer-Galley, Samira Shaikh, Sarah Taylor and Nick Webb. 2010. Modeling Socio-Cultural Phenomena in Discourse. In the Proceedings of the 23rd International Conference on Computational Linguistics (COLING-2010), Beijing, China.

Tomek Strzalkowski, George Aaron Broadwell, Sarah Taylor, Laurie Feldman, Boris Yamrom, Samira Shaikh, Ting Liu, Kit Cho, Umit Boz, Ignacio Cases and Kyle Elliott. 2013. Robust extraction of metaphor from novel data. In *Proceedings of the First Workshop on Metaphor in NLP, NAACL*. Atlanta.

Janyce Wiebe, Theresa Wilson and Claire Cardie. 2005. Annotating expressions of opinions and emotions in language. Journal of Language Resources and Evaluation 39(2-3):165–210

Yorick, Wilks. 1975. Preference semantics. *Formal Semantics of Natural Language*, E. L. Keenan, Ed. Cambridge University Press, Cambridge, U.K., 329–348.

Yorick Wilks, Lucian Galescu, James Allen, Adam Dalton. 2013. Automatic Metaphor Detection using Large-Scale Lexical Resources and Conventional Metaphor Extraction. In the *Proceedings of the First Workshop on Metaphor in NLP, (NAACL)*. Atlanta.

Chinese CogBank: Where to See the Cognitive Features of Chinese Words

Bin Li[*,†] **Xiaopeng Bai**[†] **Siqi Yin**[*] **Jie Xu**[*]
[*]School of Chinese Language and Literature
Nanjing Normal University
Nanjing, PR China
[†] Department of Computer Science
Brandeis University
MA, USA
libin.njnu@gmail.com, xpbai@brandeis.edu,
nnuyinsiqi@126.com, xujie.njnu@gmail.com

Abstract

Metaphor processing has been a heated topic in NLP. Cognitive properties of a word are important in metaphor understanding and generation. But data collected automatically tend to be reduced in both quantity and quality. This paper introduces CogBank a database of Chinese concepts and their associated cognitive properties. The database was constructed using simile templates to extract millions of "word-property" pairs via search engine over the World Wide Web. A method of manual check and correction was then implemented, resulting in the current CogBank database which contains 232,590 "word-property" pairs. CogBank also provides various search and visualization services for observing and comparing associations between concepts and properties.

1 Introduction

Metaphor studies in cognitive linguistics focus on the mechanisms of how metaphor works. Conceptual Metaphor Theory summarizes the types of mappings from source domain to target domain like "Time is Money" (Lakoff & Johnson, 1980). Blending Theory examines how the input spaces of two concepts blend new spaces (Fauconnier & Turner, 2003). Both theories emphasize the properties of a concept, which could be profiled in metaphor use. For example, *money* has properties of important, valuable and soulless that will help people to comprehend *time* in the metaphor. Many of these properties reflect common cognitive knowledge rather than scientific knowledge. If such cognitive properties can be collected and organized, it will benefit metaphor generation and understanding in NLP. However, manual construction of such databases could be time-consuming. In addition, the properties of concepts may vary from person to person. *Money* may have more than three properties and each property could be interpreted in different ways. This translates into three key issues to be solved: (1) How to collect as many concepts and properties as possible; (2) How to assure the properties are acceptable to native speakers; and, (3) How to evaluate the importance of the properties for a given concept.

Chinese CogBank is a database of cognitive properties of Chinese words. It has 232,590 "word-property" pairs, which consist of 82,937 words and 100,271 properties. The data were collected via Baidu.com, and adjudicated manually. Consequently, each "word-property" type has an associated frequency which can stand as a functional measure of the importance of a property.

The rest of the paper is organized as follows. Section 2 briefly reviews related work on collecting cognitive features. Section 3 introduces the construction of the Chinese CogBank. Descriptive statistics, search visualization tools of the database are presented in Sections 4 and 5. Section 6 discusses the potential applications of CogBank and the difficulties with respect to metaphor processing. Conclusions and future work are outlined in Section 7.

Proceedings of the Third Workshop on Metaphor in NLP, pages 77–86,
Denver, Colorado, June 5, 2015. ©2015 Association for Computational Linguistics

2 Related Work

Collecting the cognitive properties by hand can be tedious, time-consuming and problematic in terms of guaranteeing agreement between different annotators. Therefore corpus and web data have been taken as important resources. Kintsch (2000) collects noun-adjective pairs like "money-valuable" using Latent Semantic Analysis (LSA) from large corpora. Roncero et al. (2006) extracts noun-adjective pairs using the simile template "as adjective as noun". Using the same template, Veale & Hao (2007) collects English similes by querying Google using the nouns and adjectives in WordNet. Then the data contribute to a lexical metaphor knowledge base "sardonicus", which contains about 10,000 items of "noun-adjective" pairs. Veale et al. (2008) collects 25,000 items consisting of Chinese "noun-adjective" pairs from Google using words in HowNet. In a similar way, Jia & Yu (2009) collects Chinese similes from Baidu, yielding about 20,000 "noun-property" pairs.

At this stage, collection of "concept-property" pairs seems to reach a bottleneck in that it becomes difficult to substantially increase the number of valid items. The store of raw data collected is massive, ordinarily amounting to millions of items. Obviously, stores of data this massive contain much noise. Consulting each word in a normal dictionary would be a simple and efficient way to filter out noisy data. However the cost of such an approach would be that many good candidates are eliminated as they are not in the dictionary. Using a larger dictionary offers only limited improvement because many good candidates consist of multi-word expressions like "as sly as **jungle cat**", or even appear as embedded clauses such as "(Someone who is) as sly as **a fox is cunning and experienced**". Due to such difficulties, a large cognitive database is currently not available.

In addition, previous implementations have given little importance to word-property frequencies. It is important for a metaphor processing system to know how strong the relationship between the concept and the property. If the system must generate a metaphor expressing something that is white, it could find the most relevant concepts like snow and paper using collocation frequencies.

3 Construction of the Chinese CogBank

Like Roncero et al. (2006), Veale et al. (2008) and Jia & Yu (2009), we use simile templates to collect Chinese "word-property" items by querying the search engine Baidu. The lexicon items in HowNet are used to fill the simile templates.

3.1 Lexical Resources

HowNet is a structured Chinese-English bilingual lexical resource (Dong & Dong, 2006). Different from the synsets in WordNet (Miller, 1990), it describes a word by a set of structured semantic features named "sememe". About 2200 sememes are used to define 95,000 Chinese words and 85,000 English words in HowNet (ver. 2007). For example, the Chinese noun 猪(zhu) is translated to hog, pig and swine in English. The definition of 猪(zhu) is the sememe *livestock|牲畜*. A sememe is an English-Chinese combined label and is organized in a hierarchy. *livestock|牲畜 has its* hypernym sememe *animal|兽* and higher hypernym sememes *AnimalHuman|动物*, *animate|生物*, etc.

3.2 Data Collection

In Chinese, there are three simile templates which can be used to obtain the "word-property" pairs: "像 (as) + NOUN + 一样 (same)", "像 (as) + VERB + 一样 (same)" and "像 (as) + 一样 (same) + ADJ". We populated these with 51,020 nouns, 27,901 verbs and 12,252 adjectives from HowNet to query Baidu (www.baidu.com). Different from Veale et al. (2008), we included verbs because verbs as well as nouns have concept properties. For example, "抽筋(cramp)" is a verb in Chinese. It has the property "疼(painful)", which refers to people's experience in a cramp.

We submit 91,173 queries to Baidu, allowing up to 100 returned results for each query. Then 1,258,430 types (5,637,500 tokens) of "word-adjective" pairs are collected. Within such a large data set there will be many incoherent pairs. We filter out such pairs automatically via the nouns, verbs and adjectives in HowNet, resulting in a remaining 24,240 pairs. The words cover 6,022 words in HowNet, and the properties cover 3,539 words in HowNet. The high quality of these remaining pairs provides the potential for interesting results. With the frequency information, we can see the top 10 most frequent pairs that fit the intuition of Chinese native speakers (see Table 1).

ID	Word	Property	Freq
1	苹果 apple	时尚 fashionable	1445
2	呼吸 breath	自然 natural	758
3	晨曦 sun rise	朝气蓬勃 spirited	750
4	纸 paper	薄 thin	660
5	雨点 rain drop	密集 dense	557
6	自由 freedom	美丽 beautiful	543
7	雪 snow	白 white	521
8	花儿 flower	美丽 beautiful	497
9	妖精 spirit	温柔 gentle	466
10	大海 sea	深 deep	402

Table 1. Top10 Most Frequent Word-Property Pairs

It might be surprising to see that "苹果 apple-时尚 fashionable" ranks top of all pairs. However, it makes sense because Apple (the brand) products are popular in China. "妖精 spirit" often refers to a young female demon/spirit who seduces people in Chinese fairy tales. The remaining 8 words represent ordinary things people experience in everyday life.

3.3 Manual Data Check

It is painful that in 5 million raw data only 24,240 pairs are left when filtered by HowNet. As stated in Section 2, we find a more productive way to increase the quantity of the database is to manually check the original data item by item.

To that end, we develop a set of guidelines for adjudication. We obtain four types of pairs from the sentences in the raw data. First, phrases like "as lazy as pig" contain good pairs, which we tagged as NORMAL. Second, pairs from phrases like "as valuable as ash" are tagged as IRONY. Third, pairs from sentences like "as soon as possible", "as fast as I can" are tagged as ELSE. The last type is ERROR in sentences like "as lazy as…".

After the manual correction, 843,086 pairs are left. As shown in Table 2, 232,590 are NORMAL items, 1,351 are IRONY. The rate of IRONY is much lower than the English data collected by Veale & Hao (2007). The reason is not clear yet. It may due to the different simile templates used in two languages. The other two categories ELSE and ERROR are uninformative for present purposes. But we find some important phenomena in the results that will be introduced in section 4.2.

Type	Num	Example
NORMAL	232,590	as lazy as pig
IRONY	1351	as valuable as ash
ELSE	389639	as soon as possible
ERROR	219506	as lazy as…
SUM	843,086	

Table 2. Four Kinds of Word-Property Pairs

4 Statistics

We find the results after adjudication to be better in both quality and quantity, generating 232,590 NORMAL pairs as the basis of the Chinese CogBank. In this section, we discuss the differences between the method of adjudication and automatic filtering of the data. We also present the descriptive statistics of CogBank.

4.1 Statistics of CogBank

Chinese CogBank has 232,590 "word-property" pairs, which consists of 82,937 words and 100,271 properties. The words cover 7,910 HowNet words, and the properties cover 4,376 HowNet words. This indicates that many more words and properties are gathered. Here we examine how much the results change compared to the filtered data in Section 3.2. Table 3 shows the top10 most frequent word-property pairs in CogBank. The result is not substantially different. The first item has changed to "freedom-beautiful", but "apple-fashionable" still ranks high in the database. Notably, the most frequent pairs are quite similar across automatic filtering and manual data check. In other words, if one only cares about the most frequent items from the web, automatic filtering is a fast and accurate method.

ID	Word	Property	Freq
1	自由 freedom	美丽 beautiful	3285
2	铁轨 rail track	长 long	2333
3	纸 paper	薄 thin	1828
4	天使 angel	美丽 beautiful	1766
5	苹果 apple	时尚 fashionable	1764
6	妖精 spirit	温柔 gentle	1565
7	阳光 sunlight	温暖 warm	1389
8	梦 dream	自由 free	1384
9	水晶 crystal	透明 clear	1336
10	雪 snow	白 white	1210

Table 3. Top10 Most Frequent Word-Property Pairs

Next we explore what the most frequent words and properties are in Chinese CogBank. This is important as we could learn what the most common entities are that people tend to use as vehicles in similes, and the most common properties people prefer to express in everyday life. As shown in Table 4, nouns like *flower, man, water, child, human, cat, angel, wolf* and *sunshine* rank the highest in the database. These words are quite common in everyday life and they have hundreds of properties. But the top 10 properties of each word dominate more than half the occurrences of these words when employed in a simile. This indicates that people always rely more heavily on a word's salient properties to form a simile expression.

Word	# of Pros	Freq	Top 10 Properties
花儿 flower	254	16991	绽放 bloom_7809,开放 bloom_1729,美丽 beautiful_1202, 红 red_965, 盛开 bloom_681, 美 beautiful/pretty_591, 灿烂 effulgent_561, 开 bloom_436, 香 sweet_278,简单 simple_220
花 flower	268	16602	绽放 bloom_6419,盛开 bloom_5375,美丽 beautiful_864, 美 beautiful/pretty _509, 开 bloom_435, 灿烂 effulgent_391, 开放 bloom_353, 多 numerous_148, 飘舞 dance in wind_125,漂亮 beautiful_92
男人 man	758	14708	战斗 fight_8771,奋斗 strive_975,拼命 desperate_234, 坚强 strong_213, 踢球 play football_130, 挑 pick_115, 活着 live_110, 打球 play ball_105, 裸上身 half naked_102,恋爱 in love_95
水 water	884	11837	流 flow_1786,流淌 flowing_697,流动 flow_524, 稀 dilute_380, 流过 flowing_323, 透明 limpid_245, 温柔 gentle_183, 清澈 limpid_176, 清淡 mild_170,泼 splash_168
孩子 child	1642	10866	快乐 happy_420, 哭 cry_352, 天真 childlike/innocent_332, 无助 helpless_233,说真话 tell the truth_229, 哭泣 cry/weep_216,好奇 curious_197, 兴奋 excited_172,笑 smile_167,开心 happy_166
人 human	1482	9468	活着 live_609,穿衣服 wear clothe_430, 生活 live_336,思考 think_316,直立行走 bipedalism/walk upright_315, 活 live_310, 说话 speak/talk_284, 走路 walk_222, 站立 stand_188, 站 stand_135
猫 cat	828	6989	蜷缩 curl_256,可爱 cute/lovely147,蹭 rub_137, 慵懒 lazy_136, 温顺 meek_133,无声无息 silent/quiet_126, 贴心 intimate_116, 优雅 elegant/graceful_113, 懒 lazy_112, 蜷 curl_109
天使 angel	291	6461	堕落 fall_1902,美丽 beautiful_1766,守护 guard_302, 飞翔 fly_301, 可爱 lovely_296,飞 fly_241,纯洁 pure_188, 坠落 fall_72,美好 beautiful_67,漂亮 beautiful_59
狼 wolf	493	6062	嚎叫 howl_792,凶狠 fierce_699,战斗 fight_450, 思考 think_310, 嚎 howl_262, 扑 rush/attack_143, 阴狠 baleful_142,牢牢守住目标 hold the target_136,叫 howl_102,恶 fierce_99
阳光 sunshine	286	4987	温暖 warm_1389, 灿烂 bright/shining_986,包围 surround_562, 照耀 shine_296, 普照 shine_148, 洒 shine_136,明媚 sunny/shining_127,耀眼 radiant/glare_106,透明 clear_101,照亮 shine_63

Table 4. Top 10 Most Frequent Words in CogBank

Table 5 shows the most frequent properties in CogBank: *beautiful*, *bloom*, *fight*, *fly*, *convenient*, *warm*, and *painful*. Each property is associated with hundreds of words. But the frequency of the top 10 concept words occupies more than half the occurrences. This indicates that people is tend to use the same kinds of vehicles to form a simile expression.

Prop	# of Words	Freq	Top 10 Words
美丽 beautiful	816	17383	自由 free_3285,天使 angel_1766,花儿 flower_1202,花 flower_864,美玉 jade_843,嫦娥 Chang E_795,天神 god_342,凤凰羽毛 phoenix feather_283,彩虹 rainbow_260,首都金边 Phnom Penh_242
绽放 bloom	152	16150	花儿 flower_7809,花 flower_6419,花朵 bloom_269,鲜花 flower_235,莲花 lotus_149, 玫瑰 rose_108, 昙花 epiphyllum_106, 蓝玫瑰 blue rose_85,烟花 fireworks_76,玫瑰花 rose_57
战斗 fight	217	13536	男人 man_8771,英雄 hero_547,艾薇儿 Avril_473, 狼 wolf_450, 战士 soldier_295, 熊 bear_229, 爷们 menfolk_145,保尔 Pual_118,斯巴达克 Spartacus_108,勇士 warrior_99
飞 fly	375	12409	鸡毛 chicken feather_2298, 子弹 bullet_1427, 蝴蝶 butterfly_890, 鸟 bird_769,小鸟 birdie/dickey_657,箭 arrow_522, 鸟儿 bird_453, 风筝 kite_380,叶子 leaf/foliage_372,雪片 snowflake_322
简单 simple	916	8133	涂指甲油 nail polish_757, 火焰 flame_328,呼吸 breathing_231,花儿 flower_220, 打开冰箱 open the fridge_200, 吃饭 eat_188, 拉屎 shit_138,骑单车 cycling_131,遛狗 walk the dog_118,孩子 child/kid_115
盛开 bloom	68	6970	花 flower_5375,花儿 flower_681,鲜花 flower_259,蔷薇 rose_105,花朵 bloom_96,烟花 fireworks_72,向日葵 sunflower_32, 桃花 peach blos-

			som_30, 樱花 sakura_26, 恶之花 flowers of evil_24
方便 con-venient	625	5988	存款 deposit_388,电脑登录 login by computer_331, 控制电灯 control lamps_188,地铁 metro_143,取存款 withdraw_136,加油 refuel_131,取款 withdraw_129, 公交 bus_122, 家 home_118,公交车 bus_96
温暖 warm	289	5374	阳光 sunshine/sunlight_1389, 家 home_1207, 太阳 sun_535, 春天 spring_492,春风 spring breeze_132, 火炕 heated kang_109,爱情 love_98, 火 fire_77, 家庭 family_65, 拥抱 embrace/hug_61
痛 painful	479	5142	针扎 needle hit_1294, 抽筋 cramp_453,针刺 acupuncture_414,痛经 dysmenorrhea_314,刀割 cut with knife_284,散了架 fall apart_140,来月经 menstruate_102,死 die_98,火烧 burned_80,抽经 cramp_63
飞翔 fly	129	5014	鸟 bird_1290,鸟儿 bird_883,落叶 defoliation_505,鹰 eagle_410,小鸟 birdie/dickey_315,天使 angel_301,蝴蝶 butterfly_97,飞鸟 bird_89,雄鹰 eagle_70,风筝 kite_70

Table 5. Top 10 Most Frequent Properties in CogBank

4.2 Valuable Information from Uninformative Data

The manual data check drops many uninformative data which on the surface seem to possess no value, for example, "as stupid as ***you***", "as cheap as ***before***". The pronouns and time expressions have to be removed from CogBank. But through observing all the pronouns and time expressions through manual data check, we find something useful in Chinese sentences "X 像 (as) Y 一样 (same) A" (X is as A as Y) where Y is the reference object. As Indicated in Table 6, people prefer to use *我(I)* as the reference object rather than other pronouns.

Pronoun	# of Props	Freq
我 I	21962	54353
你 you	8422	20056
他 he	5678	12908
他们 they	3829	10315
她 she	2915	6576
我们 we	2583	5845
自己 self	1268	2537
别人 somebody else	1128	2291
其他人 others	1117	2437
你们 you pl.	1044	2124
它 it	519	1234
它们 they[-animate]	184	381

Table 6. Most Frequent Pronouns in Raw Data

People also prefer to reference recurring and concurrent time frames over past or future ones. As shown in Table 7, *usual (往常,平时)* occurs more than *past* and *before*, while *future(未来)* occurs with even lower frequencies.

Rank	Time	# of Props	Freq
1	往常 usual	18077	42895
2	现在 now	2320	5837
3	以往 before	2264	4563
4	从前 before	2263	4881
5	平时 usual	1705	3776
6	上次 last time	1584	3837
7	过去 past	1434	3431
8	今天 today	1124	2175
9	往年 years before	973	2179
10	往日 days before	775	1767
32	未来 future	19	557
37	明天 tomorrow	13	364

Table 7. Most Frequent Time Words in Raw Data

The usage patterns showing much higher frequencies for the pronoun *我(I)* and time expression *往常, 平时(usual)* suggest that people prefer to use their experienced everyday life knowledge to make simile or contrast sentences. This finding supports the Embodied Cognition Philosophy (Lakoff & Johnson 1980; Lakoff 2008), which hypothesizes that much of our conceptual structure is based on knowledge formed through physical and emotional experience.

Work on this kind of knowledge is still in its preliminary stage, and presents the potential to advance smarter automatic metaphor generation and QA systems.

5 Online Search and Visualization

The web version[1] of Chinese CogBank provides basic and visualized searches. Users can search for the properties of a particular concept or the concepts associated with a specific property. We also developed a search service for English users. An English word like *snow* will be translated into Chinese first with HowNet, and then the system will show its properties with English translations.

The above search services are provided in ordinary table form. We also use the Visualization

[1] http://cognitivebase.com/

Toolkit D3[2] (Bostock, 2011) to draw dynamic graphs for the search results. The functions are listed as follows.

(1) Generate the graph of properties for a given word. Or generate the graph of words for a given property.
(2) Generate a graph comparing properties for given words. Or generate a graph comparing words for given properties.
(3) Generate the extended graph of properties for a given word. The graph is extended by the words for the properties. Or generate the extended graph of words for a given property. The graph is extended by the properties for the words.
(4) Generate the graph of properties for a given word with sememes in HowNet.
(5) Generate the graph of properties for a given English word with translation by HowNet and extended by the sememes in HowNet.

Appendixes A-E illustrate the visualization graphs. Due to the copyright of HowNet, functions (4) and (5) have not been made available online. Many more visualization functions are currently under development. We hope these online services will help linguistic researchers and second language learners with their studies.

6 Discussion

Veale (2014) argues that such knowledge is useful for metaphor, irony, humor processing and sentiment extraction. The cognitive database with a large store of properties will be useful for both linguistics and NLP. Nevertheless, we still face many challenges in developing a metaphor processing system. We now discuss some of the problems in using such a resource in NLP.

(1) Cognitive properties cannot be used directly in simile and irony generation. It seems straight forwards but there are many complicated aspects of simile sentence generation. For example, if we want to generate a simile sentence to express that someone is very tall, we could simply query CogBank for the words having tall properties. Then we find words like *mountain, hill, tree, giraffe,* etc. We may say "Tom is as tall as a giraffe". But it's odd to say "Tom is as tall as a mountain" or "Tom is taller than a mountain" unless in fairy tales. However, when we want to express some building is very tall, we would choose mountain and hill but not giraffe. If we say "the building is as high as a giraffe", it is more likely to be an ironic statement. So it's obvious that the tenor in the sentence will influence or restrict the choice of vehicle. In simile generation, scientific world knowledge seems indispensable.

(2) Cognitive properties alone are not sufficient in metaphor understanding. If one says "Tom is a pig", we have to indicate whether it is a metaphor or not. If it is, the cognitive properties will supply the candidate ground of the metaphor. The problem is that there are so many properties that the ground may vary in different contexts. Sometimes it is "greedy", and sometimes it is "fat". Reconciling such ambiguity and contextual dependency requires a dynamic model for the context.

To sum up, there is still much work to be done before we are able to completely integrate cognitive word knowledge in language processing systems.

7 Conclusion and Future Work

In this paper, we introduced the construction of Chinese CogBank which contains 232,590 items of "word-property" pairs. Querying search engines with simile templates is a fast and efficient way to obtain a large number of candidate pairs. But to increase the quantity and quality of the database, manual check and adjudication are necessary. Using CogBank we identified interesting preferences people exhibit during production of similes in natural language. We also established multiple online search and visualization services for public use.

In the future, we will make further investigate of the CogBank's raw and labelled data. Second, we will compare the cognitive features across languages. Third, we will try to adapt CogBank for deployment in Chinese metaphor processing systems.

Acknowledgments

We are grateful for the extensive and constructive comments provided by the blind peer reviewers. We are especially thankful to Patricia Lichtenstein for the proofread revision. This work was supported in part by National Social Science Fund of China under contract 10CYY021, 11CYY030 and

[2] http://d3js.org/

Qing Lan Project Fund of Nanjing Normal University.

References

Dong, Z. D. & Dong, Q. 2006. *HowNet and the Computation of Meaning*. Singapore, World Scientific Press.

Fauconnier G., Turner. 2003. *The Way We Think: Conceptual Blending and The Mind's Hidden Complexities*. Basic Books.

Jia Y. X. and Yu S. W. 2009. Instance-based Metaphor Comprehension and Generation. *Computer Science*, 36(3):138-41.

Kintsch, W. 2000. Metaphor comprehension: A computational theory. *Psychonomic Bulletin & Review*, Vol. 7: 257-66.

Lakoff, G. & Johnson. M. 1980. *Metaphors We Live by*. Chicago: The University of Chicago Press.

Lakoff, G. 2008. *Philosophy in the Flesh*. Basic Books.

Bostock M., Ogievetsky V., Heer J. 2011. D3: Data-Driven Documents. *IEEE Trans. Visualization & Comp. Graphics*, Vol. 17(12):2301-2309.

Miller, G. A., R. Beckwith, C. D. Fellbaum, D. Gross, K. Miller. 1990. WordNet: An online lexical database. *Int. J. Lexicograph*. 3, 4:235-244.

Roncero, C., Kennedy, J. M., and Smyth, R. 2006. Similes on the internet have explanations. *Psychonomic Bulletin and Review*, 13(1).

Veale, T. & Hao, Y. F. 2007. Learning to Understand Figurative Language: From Similes to Metaphors to Irony. *Proceedings of CogSci 2007*, Nashville, USA.

Veale, T., Hao, Y. and Li, G. 2008. Multilingual Harvesting of Cross-Cultural Stereotypes. *Proceedings of ACL 2008*, Ohio, USA.

Veale, T. 2014. A Service-Oriented Architecture for Metaphor Processing. In *Proceedings of the Second Workshop on Metaphor in NLP*, ACL 2014.

Appendix

A. The graph of properties of 猪(pig).

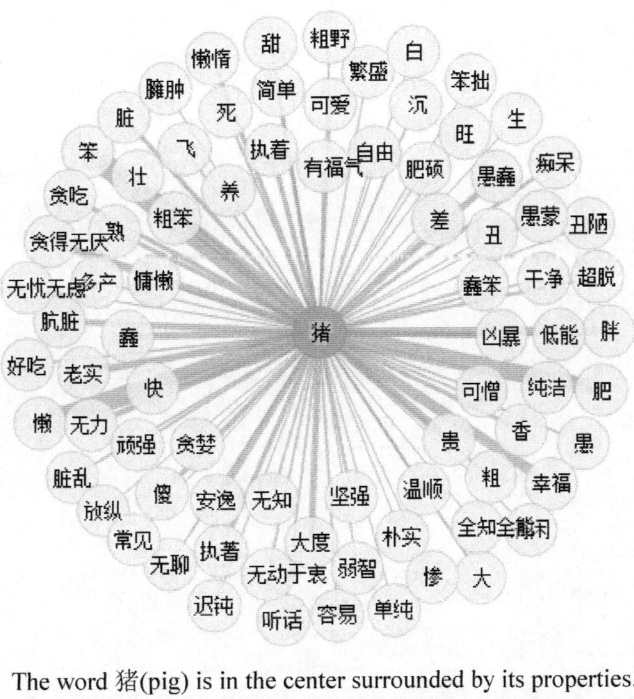

The word 猪(pig) is in the center surrounded by its properties.
The width of the line indicates the frenqucies of the "word-property" pairs.

B. The comparison graph of 猪(pig), 猫(cat) and 狗(dog).

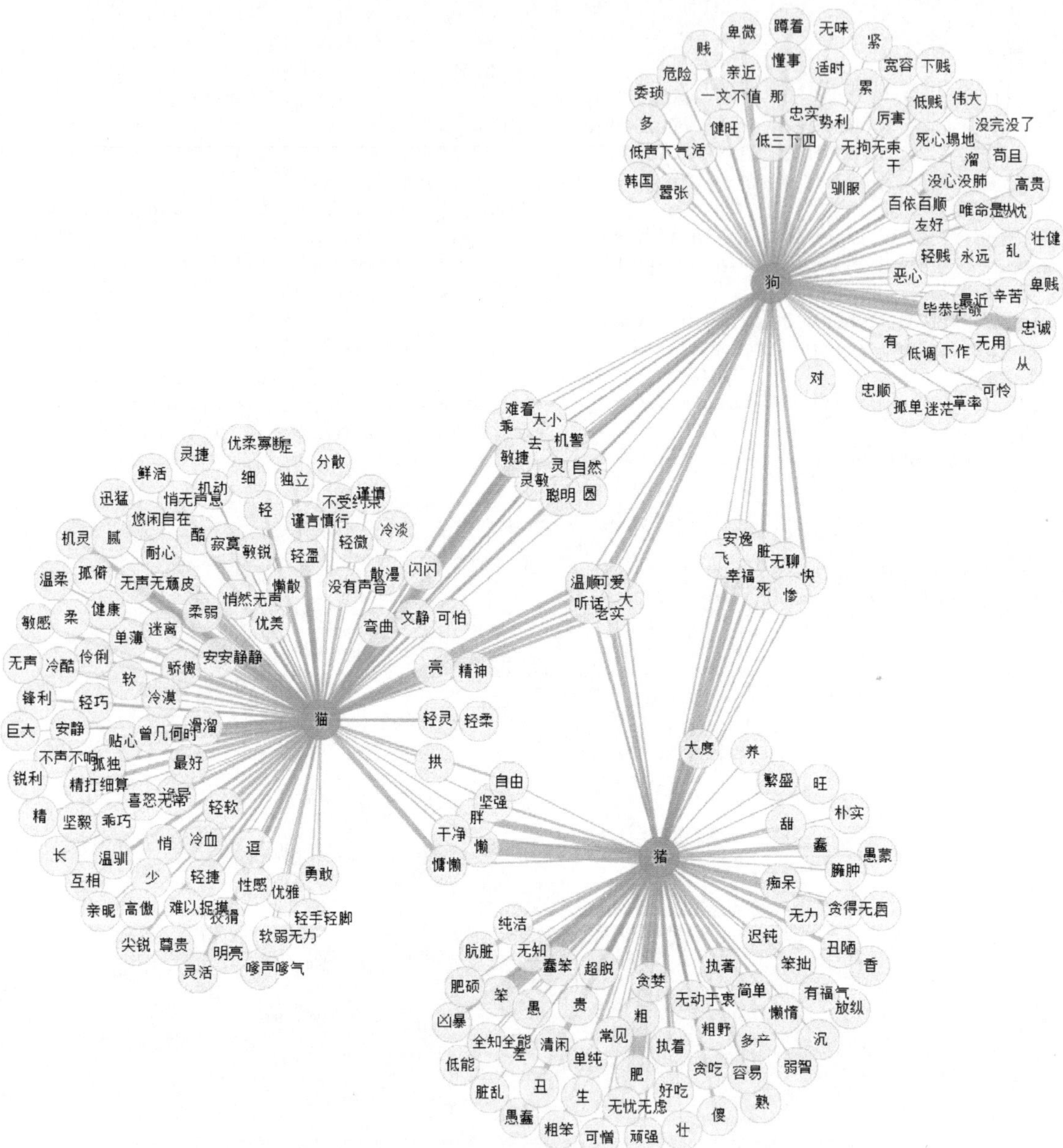

The 猪(pig), 猫(cat) and 狗(dog) share some properties.

C. The visualized graph of 猪(pig) with extensions by the propeties of 猪(pig).

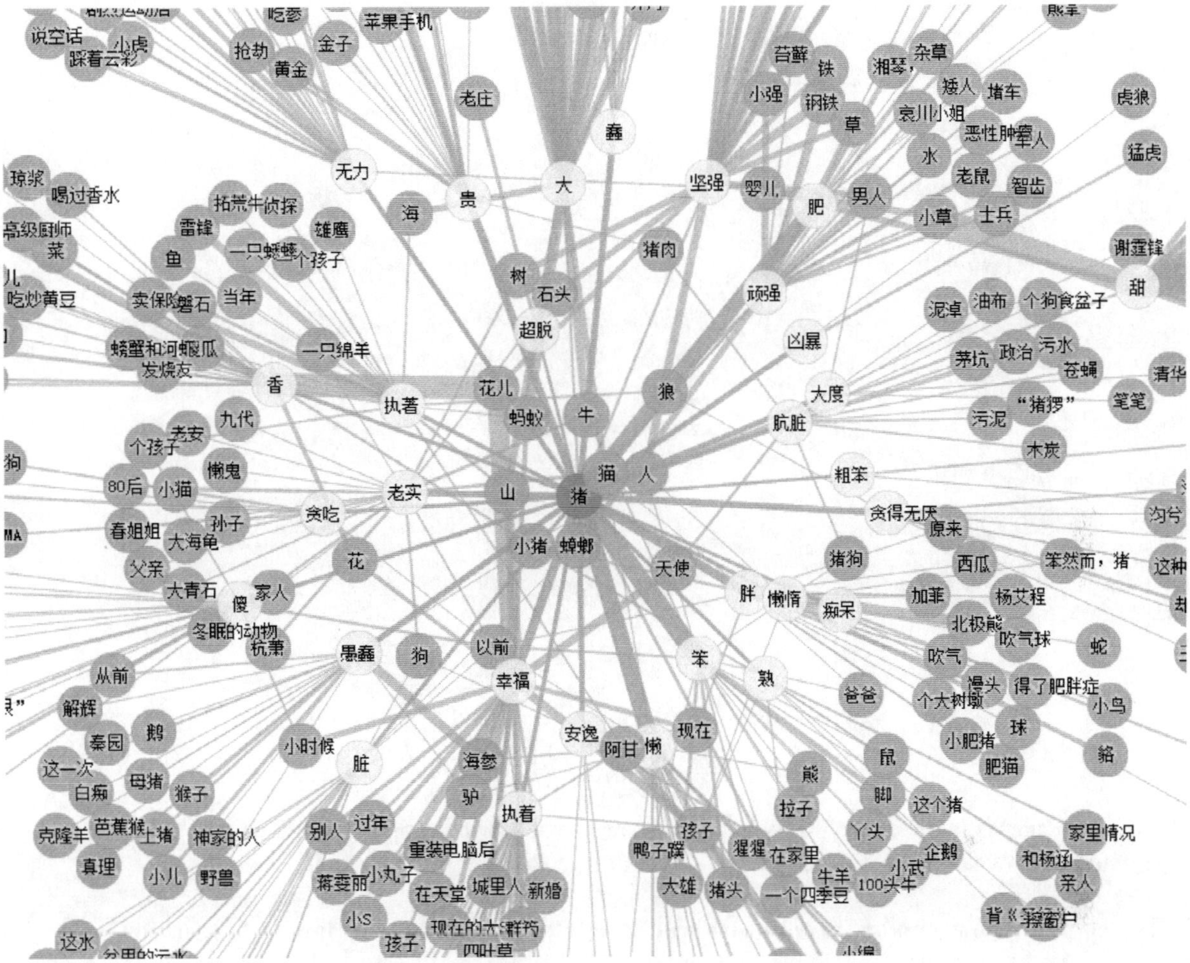

The 猪(pig) has many properties(yellow nodes), and these yellow nodes have their words(orange nodes). So the extendted orange nodes share more properites with 猪(pig) appear closer to the center.

D. The visualized graph of 猪(pig) with bilingual sememe labels from HowNet.

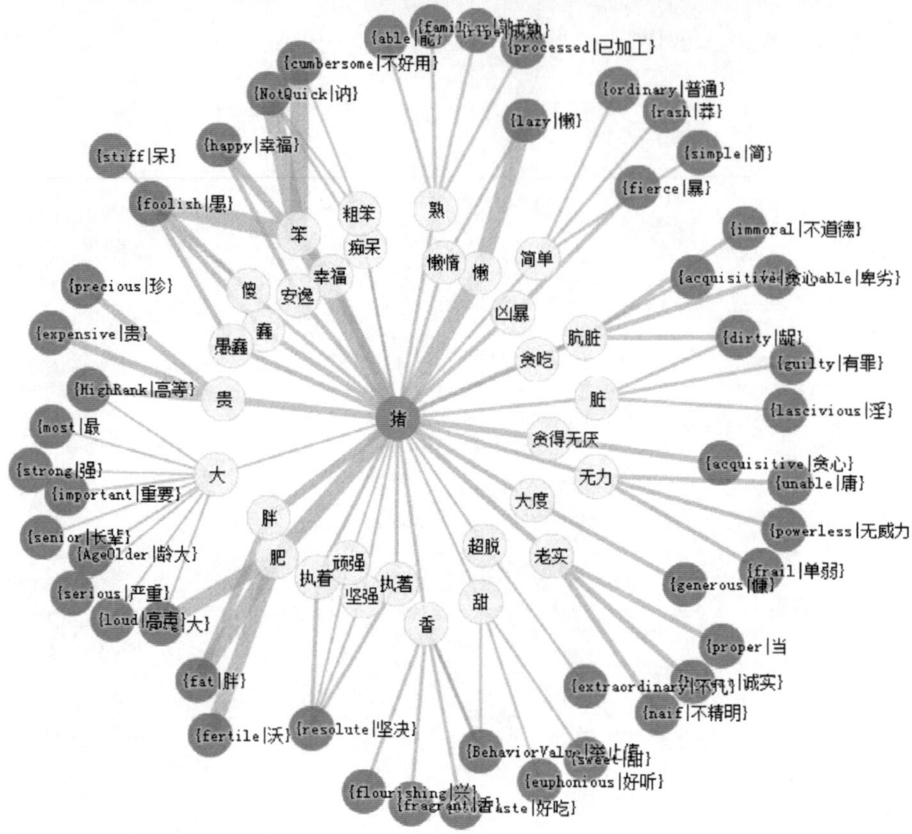

The word 猪(pig) is in the center surrounded by its properties. Each property is linked to a bilingual sememe in HowNet (blue nodes).

E. The comparison graph of "sheep" with translation "羊" extended by HowNet's sememes.

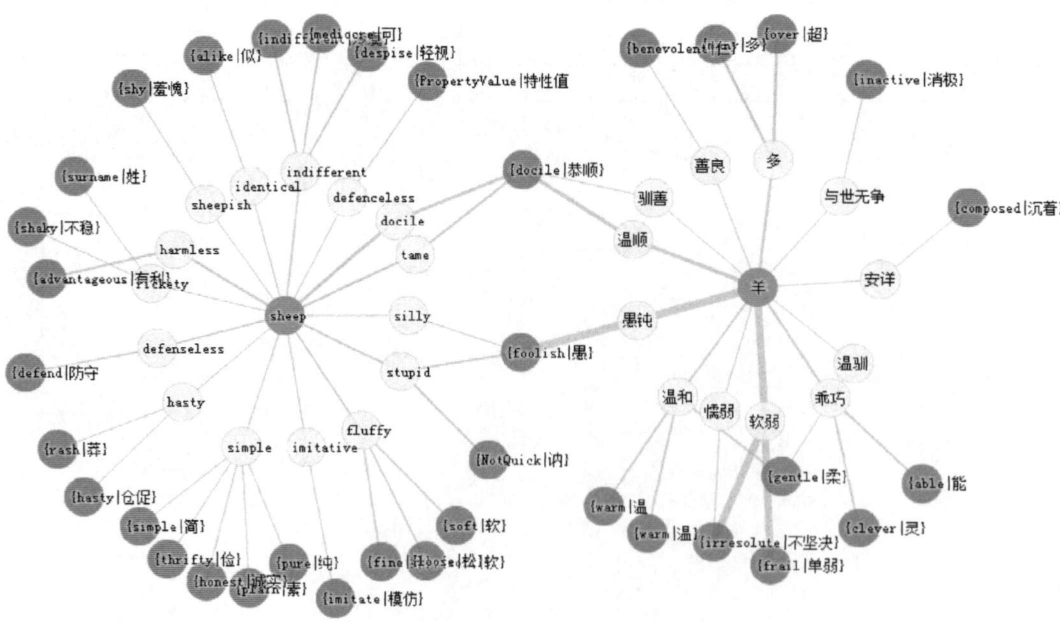

Fighting Words and Antagonistic Worlds

Tony Veale
School of Computer Science and Informatics
University College Dublin
Belfield, Dublin D4, Ireland.
Tony.Veale@UCD.ie

Abstract

Metaphor is a fundamentally antagonistic way of viewing and describing the world. Metaphors ask us to see what is *not* there, so as to remake the world to our own liking and to suit our own lexicons. But if metaphors clash with the world as it is, they can also clash with each other. Each metaphor represents a stance from which to view a topic, and though some stances are mutually compatible, many more are naturally opposed to each other. So while we cringe at a clumsily mixed metaphor, there is real value to be had from a deliberate opposition of conceptual metaphors. Such contrasts reveal the limits of a particular worldview, and allow us to extract humorous insight from each opposition. We present here an automatic approach to the framing of antagonistic metaphors, embodied in a metaphor-generating Twitterbot named @*MetaphorMagnet*.

1 Two-Fisted Metaphors

The imagination often takes flight on the wings of metaphor. For metaphor allows us to make the fantastical seem real and the banal seem fresh and newly interesting. For example, consider this imaginary scenario, as packaged in a pithy tweet:

What if #TheXMen were real? #NoamChomsky could be its #ProfessorCharlesXavier: smart yet condescending, and scowling too

This counterfactual injects some much-needed pizzazz into the banalities of modern politics and intellectual posturing, by reimagining a famously dour academic activist as the real-world equivalent of a much-loved comic-book character. This counterfactual is, at its heart, a metaphor: we can construct a bridge from *Chomsky* to *Xavier* only because we believe them to share deep similarities. If the metaphor implies much more than this set of properties actually conveys, this is because it also sparks the imagination of its audience. We are lead to imagine Chomsky as the cerebral hero of a battle between good and evil, in which he leads his own academic version of the X-Men, loyal students with a zealous sense of mission.

Now consider this follow-up tweet, which is designed to further stoke a reader's imagination:

If #NoamChomsky is just like #ProfessorCharlesXavier, smart yet condescending, then who in #TheXMen is #GeorgeLakoff most like?

Metaphors are systematic, and lead us to project coherent systems of relational structure from one domain to another (see Lakoff & Johnson, 1980; Gentner *et al.*, 1989). In this way we invent hybrid worlds that combine elements of reality *and* fantasy, in which each mapping, such as Chomsky to Xavier, can prompt others, such as Lakoff to his mutant counterpart (Magneto, perhaps?).

The real world is not a comic book, and there is something mischievously silly about describing a serious scholar and activist as a fictional creation with super-powers. Yet metaphors work well as jokes when they make a virtue of the differences that separate ideas. As Pollio (1996) put it, "*split reference yields humour if the joined items (or the act joining them) emphasize the boundary or line separating them; split reference yields metaphor if the boundary between the joined items (or the act joining them) is obliterated and the two items fuse to form a single entity.* So by dialing up the antagonism – between domains, between reality and

Proceedings of the Third Workshop on Metaphor in NLP, pages 87–94,
Denver, Colorado, June 5, 2015.

fantasy, or between people and ideas – a metaphor can yield a witty, eye-catching and thought-provoking text that is worth sharing on a platform such as Twitter. This point is worth stressing, as the above tweets were generated by an automated *Twitterbot*, named @MetaphorMagnet, whose antagonism-stoking generative processes are the subject of this paper.

If metaphor can give you wings, it can also give you fists with which to pummel a contrary point of view. Every conceptual metaphor offers a potted world-view that encourages us to reason in certain ways, and thus speak in related ways, about our experiences. But like proverbs, or indeed ideologies, we can often pick and choose the ones that suit us best. Reasonable people can disagree about how best to categorize a situation, as no metaphor is ever objectively right or true, just potentially apt in a particular context. Thus, thinkers on different ends of the political spectrum offer antagonistic metaphors to frame the same goals, needs or problems, and by advancing their own conceptual frames they actively seek to undermine those of their opponents. Just as every proverb has a converse that is equally compelling (e.g., *many hands make light work* vs. *too many cooks spoil the broth*), there is conceptual sport to be had in finding the most apt *anti*-metaphor for a given figurative viewpoint. The following tweet thus frames two antagonistic views of *love*:

To some beatniks, love is a sparkling rainbow. To others, it is a flat bed.
#Love=#Rainbow #Love=#Bed

This tweet nicely captures the antagonism that exists between competing perspectives on #Love. The first is expansive, and views love as a many-splendored thing; the second is more reductive, and views love as just a means to an end: *sex*. By attributing these views to different members of the same category of person – *beatniks* – the tweet suggests that this conflict of ideas is also a conflict between otherwise similar people.

This paper explores the automated generation of antagonistic metaphors. By elevating simple contrasts into a contest of ideas, @Metaphor Magnet creates metaphors that also work as witty provocations to think differently, or at least to appreciate the limits of received wisdom. This automated system seeks its inspiration in attested usage data and uses a variety of knowledge-rich services to produce elaborate, well-reasoned metaphors that hinge upon meaningful contrasts. In the sections that follow, we describe how this harmonious marriage of explicit knowledge and raw usage data is used to sow disharmony at the level of ideas and package the results as tweets.

2 Competing Points of View

A divergent problem is one that admits many potential solutions, each of them valid in its own way (Guilford, 1967). Though one may be privileged over others by its conventionality – e.g. the use of a brick as a building block, or of a paper clip to bind papers – there is no single, objectively *correct* answer. Conversely, a convergent problem is one that admits just one objectively-acceptable *correct* answer, relative to which all others are seen as deficient or just plain *wrong*. By this standard, metaphor is a divergent approach to the conveyance of meaning, while literal language – to the extent that any text can be truly literal – is considerably more convergent.

A cornerstone of divergent thinking is divergent categorization: this allows us to categorize a familiar object or idea in atypical ways that permit new and unusual uses for it (Torrance, 1980). Such categorization is, in turn, central to the act of figurative description. Consider the metaphor *divorce is war*, whose interpretation requires us to find a non-trivial category – one a good deal more specific than *event* – to embrace these very different-seeming concepts (Glucksberg, 1998). To see how people categorize, we need only see how they speak. On the Web, we see descriptions of both war and of divorce, in separate texts, as *traumatic events*, *serious conflicts*, *immoral acts*, and as *bad things* in general. Such descriptions often come in standardized linguistic containers, such as the "*A_Bs such as Cs*" pattern of Hearst (1992), instances of which are easily harvested from the Web. The *Thesaurus Rex* Web service of Veale & Li (2013) offers up its resulting system of Web-harvested categorizations as a public service that can be exploited by 3rd-party metaphor systems. *Thesaurus Rex* can be used for the interpretation of metaphors by permitting another system to explore specific unifying categories for distant ideas, such as *divorce & war*, but it can also be used in the generation of metaphors. So if looking for a metaphor for creativity, *Thesaurus Rex* suggests the category special ability, leading a metaphor generator to consider other members of this category as possible vehicles, such as *x-ray vision, superior strength, magic* or *prophecy*. *@MetaphorMagnet* thus uses *Thesaurus Rex* to package diverse ideas into a single tweet, as in:

> *#Take5 of the #Shallowest things:*
> *1. Toilet Bowls*
> *2. Rock Stars*
> *3. Cookie Sheets*
> *4. Soup Bowls*
> *5. Rush Limbaugh*
> *#TheRepublicans*

Divergent thinking typically arises when we go *off-script* to imagine unconventional possibilities for a familiar object or idea. Raskin (1985) puts the concept of a script at the centre of his computational theory of jokes, the *Semantic Script Theory of Humour* (SSTH), arguing that most joke narratives are compatible with two competing scripts at once. The primary script, which listeners are lulled into applying based on a normative reading of a narrative, is activated as the result of convergent thinking; the secondary script, which the joker downplays at first and which listeners only perceive when a big "*reveal*" is delivered at the end, is a result of divergent thinking and an ability to find novel uses for familiar situations. Metaphors rely on categories the way jokes rely on scripts. Thus, while the category *immoral act* will embrace acts that are clearly immoral, such as *murder, torture, bribery* and *fraud*, in the right circumstances it can also be used to embrace the outlier ideas *divorce, drug use* and even *dancing*.

Nonetheless, the closest equivalent to a script in metaphor is the *Conceptual Metaphor* (CM). Conceptual Metaphors, as described in Lakoff & Johnson (1980), are the cognitive deep structures that underpin whole families of related linguistic metaphors. The *Life is a Journey* CM, for example, is the fountainhead of figures of speech such as "*go off the rails*", "*hit the skids*", "*crash and burn*", "*smooth sailing*" and "*on the rocks*." So just as trips to many kinds of restaurant can all be understood using a generic *Restaurant* script (i.e. *enter-sit-order-eat-pay-leave*), a CM such as *Life is a Journey* facilitates a generic level of reasoning about life's events. And just as a script has slots for various roles, props and locations, a CM has its own schematic structure with slots to fill, such as *Source, Path, Goal* and *Vehicle*. A CM such as *Life is a Journey* thus allows us to impose the schematic structure of a *Journey* onto our mental structure of a *Life*, to understand *Life* as something with a starting point, a destination, a path to follow and a means of conveyance.

Carbonell (1981), Martin (1990) and Barnden (2008) each build and exploit an explicit representation of conceptual metaphors, while Mason (2004) uses statistical methods to extract conventional metaphors – CMs that are so entrenched in the way we speak that their uses in language can often seem literal – from text corpora. Shutova (2010) uses statistical clustering to identify possible target ideas – such as *Democracy* and *Marriage* – for a given source idea such as *Mechanism*. This allows her system to recognize "*fix a marriage*" and "*the functioning of democracy*" (or vice versa) as figurative uses of a *Mechanism* schema because they each use verbs that typically take mechanisms as their objects. But whether one views CMs as real cognitive structures or as useful statistical generalizations, CMs serve as script-like bundles of norms and roles that shape the generation and interpretation of metaphors.

In any case, CMs are so often paraphrased in the metaphor literature using copula statements of the form *X is a Y* that candidate CMs are easily harvested from a source of Web n-grams, not just because the metaphor literature is itself part of the Web, but because lay speakers have over-used many of these forms to the point of cliché. So the Google n-grams (Brants & Franz, 2006) is not just a source of CM paraphrases such as "*Life is a Journey*" (freq=12,688) but of colorful variations on these themes as well, such as "*Life is a Highway*" (freq=2,443), "*Life is a Rollercoaster*" (freq=3,803), "*Life is a Train*" (freq=188), "*Life is a Maze*" (freq = 180), "*Life is a Pilgrimage*" (freq=178) and "*Life is a River*" (freq=119). If one doubts that metaphor is a divergent phenomenon, one need only look at the Google n-grams, which attests that people also speak as though "*Life is a Game*" (freq=8,763), "*Life is a Circus*" (freq=598), "*Life is a Banquet*" (freq=102), and even that "*Life is a Sitcom*" (freq=180).

These short linguistic expressions typically sit on the figurative continuum somewhere between proverbs and clichés, as such phrases must have a minimum Web frequency of 40 to ever find their way into the Google n-grams. Like clichés, these phrases crystalize a wealth of received wisdom, but just like proverbs they offer just one potted view on a topic, one that is easily countered by an apt choice of counter-proverb or anti-metaphor, as we shall show in coming sections.

3 Grudge Matches

Google 4-grams are a rich source of copula metaphors such as "*Life is an Adventure*" (freq= 1,317) and "*Life is an Illusion*" (freq=95), while the 3-grams also offer up gems such as "*Life is Rubbish*" (freq=8,489), "*Life is Love*" (freq=889) and "*Life is War*" (freq=44,490). Many of these n-grams give linguistic form to established CMs, but many more occupy a questionable area between resonant metaphor and random, overheard phrase. So a computational system must exercise careful selectivity in deciding which n-grams are worthy of elaboration into a novel linguistic form and which are best discarded as unreliable noise.

A good starting point is affect, as those copula n-grams that assert the identity of polarized ideas with antagonistic sentiments, such as *faith* and *aggression*, make for provocative metaphors. So consider the 4-gram "*faith is an aggression*" (freq=44), whose frequency is high enough to suggest it is well-formed, but low enough to suggest it resides in the long-tail of public opinion. Most sentiment lexica will view faith as a strong positive idea and aggression as a strong negative, so these ideas make for a bold juxtaposition, as packaged in this tweet from @*MetaphorMagnet:*

Remember when faiths were practiced by kind priests? Now, faith is an aggression that only unkind aggressors exhibit.

Notice that the original motivating 4-gram "*faith is an aggression*" sits at the centre of the tweet. @*MetaphorMagnet* seeks its inspiration from the Google n-grams, to find some interesting snippet of text that may, with reasoned elaboration, blossom into a fuller form that is worthy of tweeting. Viewed in this way, an n-grams database is like a crowded railway station, buzzing with fleeting morsels of overheard conversations. When one's interest is finally piqued by a particular fragment, one has no choice but to complete it oneself.

Yet reasoned elaboration demands knowledge over which a system can reason, and the tweet above showcases several pieces of stereotypical knowledge: that priests are often kind and practice faiths, while aggressors are often unkind and exhibit aggression. Knowledge of stereotypical properties is sourced as needed from *Thesaurus Rex* and from a database of typical associations mined on the Web by Veale & Hao (2007), while relational knowledge – linking e.g. priests to their faiths via specific actions – is sourced from yet another public Web service, *Metaphor Eyes,* as presented in Veale & Li (2011). The relational triples provided by *Metaphor Eyes*, mined from WH-questions commonly found in Web query logs (e.g. "*why do priests wear white collars?*"), can also be used to generate simple analogies, though the most provocative analogies are often antagonistic disanalogies. Consider an analogical tweet that @*MetaphorMagnet* tags as an #*irony*:

#Irony: When some anglers use "pointed" *hooks the way salespersons use pointless gimmicks. #Angler=#Salesperson #Hook=#Gimmick*

Each of @*MetaphorMagnet*'s tweets strives for a balance of similarity and dissimilarity. The analogical similarity here derives from a parallelism in the action of two agents – each *use something* – while the dissimilarity derives from a specific contrast between the objects so used. Though the contrast of *pointed* and *pointless* is mere wordplay, it is may be enough to spark more profound processes of meaning construction in the reader. To spur the reader into engaging these processes, the system explicitly hashtags the tweet as *ironic*, and puts the positive side of the contrast, *pointed*, in scare quotes. The reader is thus prompted to view the dissimilarity as merely superficial, and to read a deeper meaning into what is essentially a superficial similarity. The reader, if not the system, is left with the image of a bad fisherman, for whom pointed hooks are just pointless gimmicks. The use of ironic scare quotes to signal fakeness or insincerity is made more explicit in this tweet:

#Irony: When some jewelers sell "valuable" *diamonds the way tinkers sell valueless junk. #Jeweler=#Tinker #Diamond=#Junk*

So @*MetaphorMagnet* strives to sow antagonism even in the presence of unifying similarity, by for example, choosing to mold this similarity into the most negative comparisons. Consider another of the system's rendering strategies in this tweet:

Tourist. noun. A creep who would rather enjoy bizarre excursions than bizarre perversions.
#Tourist=#Creep

Once again the similarity here hinges on a rather generic shared relationship: tourists enjoy excursions and creeps enjoy perversions. The contrast is primarily one of affect: *tourist* has mildly positive sentiment as a lexical concept, while *creep* has an especially strong negative sentiment. And though *bizarre* is a stereotypical property of the concept *perversion*, the Google 2-gram "*bizarre perversion*" (freq=111) attests that speakers often apply the property *bizarre* to excursions too.

A system may go further and use hashtags to imply a similarity that borders on identity, as in:

Would you rather be:
1. A guardian supervising an innocent child?
2. A jailer supervising a culpable offender?
#Guardian=#Jailer

So while antagonistic views on the world stress the conflict between two opposing situations, we can provoke deeper antagonism still by asserting these situations to be almost identical beneath the surface. Yet the screenwriter's maxim of *show, don't tell* applies as much to tweets as it does to films, so it helps if we can do more than just *tell* of identity and actually *show* near-identicality in action. This requires some imagination, and perhaps more space than a single tweet will permit. Fortunately, bots are not limited to single tweets, and can issue two in quick succession if need be:

When it comes to the devotees they lead, some swamis can be far from mellow and can even seem authoritarian.
#Swami=#Warlord #Devotee=#Rebel

Authoritarian swamis lead hardened devotees the way warlords lead rebels.
#Swami=#Warlord #Devotee=#Rebel

So tweets, like movies, can have sequels too.

4 Counter-Punches and Anti-Metaphors

Metaphors are underspecified and often highly context-dependent, and so many of the potential CMs that are harvested from the Google n-grams are not amenable to computational interpretation. Indeed, many – though suggestive – are not truly CMs in any accepted sense, and the 4-gram "*love is a bed*" is more Conceptual Metonymy than Conceptual Metaphor, a conflation of bed with sex that underpins euphemisms such as "*in the sack*", "*between the sheets*" and "*sleep together*". A CM-like paraphrase will always mean more to humans who experience the world first-hand than to machines with basic symbolic representations. So a possible CM in isolation, such as the 4-gram "*idea is a gift*" (freq=94) or "*idea is a contradiction*" (freq=72), may present few computational opportunities to provoke deep thoughts, but opportunities for meaning construction abound if candidate CMs are placed into antagonistic juxtapositions, as in this *@MetaphorMagnet* tweet:

To some thinkers, every idea is a comforting gift. To others, every idea is a disturbing contradiction.
#Idea=#Gift #Idea=#Contradiction

The ubiquity of most CMs makes them bland and uninteresting as linguistic statements to anyone but a metaphor theorist, and so they can resemble platitudes more than true insights. But computational systems like *@MetaphorMagnet* can make generic CMs seem interesting again, by undermining their generality and revealing their limits. The key is antagonistic contrast, either between rival CMs or between a CM and literal language. Consider the conceptual metaphor that underpins the expression "*pack of girls.*" The word "*pack*" is literally used to denote a group of animals, yet its figurative extension to people is so ubiquitous in speech that we often overlook the hidden slur. This tweet reminds us that it is, indeed, an insult:

To join and travel in a pack: This can turn pretty girls into ugly coyotes. #Girl=#Coyote

The Google n-grams furnish the 3-grams "*pack of coyotes*" (freq=2120) and "*pack of girls*" (freq =745"). This is as close as the system comes to the underlying CM, but it is enough to establish a parallel that facilitates a provocative contrast. Ultimately, the only pragmatics that @MetaphorMagnet needs is the pragmatics of provocation.

5 And In The Red Corner …

The notion that one CM can have an antagonistic relationship to another is itself just a metaphor, for antagonism is a state of affairs that can only hold between people. So to dial up the figurative antagonism to 11 and turn it into something approaching the real thing, we might imagine the kinds of people that espouse the views inherent to conflicting CMs, and thereby turn a contest of ideas into an intellectual rivalry between people.

On Twitter, the handles we choose can be as revealing as the texts we write and re-tweet, and so the creation of an online persona often begins with the invention of an apt new name. For instance, we might expect a *beatnik* (to recall our earlier figurative tweet from @*MetaphorMagnet*) with the handle @rainbow_lover to agree with the general thrust of the CM *Love is a Rainbow*. Conversely, what better handle for an imaginary champion of the metaphor *Love is a Rainbow* than @rainbow_lover? To condense a CM into a representative Twitter handle such as this, we can look to the Google 2-grams for suggestions. Consider the CM *Alcohol is a Drug*; while many may see this as literal truth, it is mined as a likely CM by @*MetaphorMagnet* from the Google 4-gram "*Alcohol is a Drug*" (freq=337). The system learns from the *Metaphor Eyes* service that addicts abuse drugs, and finds the Google 2-gram "*alcohol addict*" (freq=1250) to attest to the well-formedness of the name @alcohol_addict. It now has an imaginary champion for this CM, which it elaborates into the following tweet:

I always thought alcohol was drunk by bloated alcoholics. But .@alcohol_addict says alcohol is a drug that only focused addicts abuse.

The same strategy – in which a CM is condensed into an attested 2-gram that integrates aspects of the source and target ideas of the metaphor – is used *twice* in the following tweet to name rival champions for two antagonistic views on life:

.@life_lover says life is a relaxing pleasure .@abortion_patient says it is a traumatic suffering #Life=#Pleasure #Life=#Suffering

Notice that in the examples above, @life_lover and @alcohol_addict turn out to be the names of real Twitter users, while no Twitter user has yet adopted the handle @*abortion_patient*. When the system invents a plausible handle for the imaginary champion of a metaphorical viewpoint, we should not be surprised if a human has already taken that name. However, as the names fit the viewpoints, we do not expect an existing Twitter user such as @alcohol_addict to take umbrage at what is a reasonable inference about their views. Indeed, names such as @alcohol_addict already incorporate a good deal of caricature and social pretense, and it is in this spirit of make-believe that @*MetaphorMagnet* re-uses them as actors.

6 The Judges' Decision

Mark Twain offered this advice to other (human) writers: "*Get your facts first, then you can distort them as you please*." It is advice that is just as applicable to metaphor-generating computational systems such as @*MetaphorMagnet* that seek to use their uncontentious knowledge of stereotypical ideas to generate provocative comparisons. Many of @*MetaphorMagnet*'s facts come from its various knowledge sources, such as the Web services *Thesaurus Rex* and *Metaphor Eyes*, as well as a large body of stereotypical associations. But many more are not "facts" about the world but observations of what people say on the Web. One might wonder then if a random sampling of @*MetaphorMagnet*'s outputs would yield tweets that are as comprehensible and interesting as the examples we have presented in this paper.

A notable benefit of implementing any metaphor-generating system as a Twitterbot is that all of the system's outputs – its hits *and* its misses – are available for anyone to scrutinize on Twitter. Nonetheless, it is worth quantifying the degree to which typical users find a system's outputs to be meaningful, novel and worth sharing with others. We thus sampled 60 of @*MetaphorMagnet*'s past tweets and gave these to paid volunteers on CrowdFlower.com to rate along the dimensions of *comprehensibility*, *novelty* and *retweetability*. Judges were paid a small fee per judgment but were not informed of the mechanical origin of any tweet; rather, they were simply told that each was taken from Twitter for its figurative content.

We solicited 10 ratings per tweet, though this number of ratings was eventually reduced once the likely scammers – unengaged judges that offer random or unvarying answers or which fail the simple tests interspersed throughout the evaluation – were filtered from the raw results set. For each dimension, judges offered a rating for a given tweet on the following scale: 1=*very low*; 2=*medium low*; 3=*medium high*; 4=*very high*. The aggregate rating for each dimension of each tweet is then calculated as the mean rating from all judges for that dimension of that tweet.

For the dimension of *comprehensibility*, over half (51.5%) of tweets are deemed to have *very-high* aggregate comprehensibility, while 23.7% are deemed to have *medium-high* comprehensibility. Only 11.6% of the system's tweets are judged to have *very low* comprehensibility, and just 13.2% have *medium low* comprehensibility.

For the dimension of *novelty*, almost half of *@MetaphorMagnet's* tweets (49.8%) are judged to exhibit *very high* aggregate novelty, while only 11.9% are judged to exhibit *very low* novelty.

For the dimension of *retweetability*, for which judges were asked to speculate about the likelihood of sharing a given tweet with one's followers on Twitter, 15.3% of tweets are deemed to have *very high* retweet value on aggregate, while 15.5% are deemed to have *very low* retweet value. Most tweets fall into the two intermediate categories: 49.9% are deemed to have *medium low* retweet value, while 27.4% are deemed to have *medium high* retweet value. Though based on speculative evaluation rather than actual retweet rates, these numbers accord with our own informal experience of the bot on Twitter, as thus far its own designers have favorited approx. 27% of the bot's ~7500 tweets to date. It should also be noted that a 15.3% retweet rate would be considered rather ambitious for most Twitter users, and is thus perhaps an overstatement in the case of *@MetaphorMagnet* too. We thus see this as a speculative but nonetheless encouraging result.

@MetaphorMagnet currently has approx. 250 human followers (as of March 1st, 2015), though it has not yet attracted enough followers to facilitate a robust empirical analysis of their rates of *favoriting* or *retweeting*. If and when it attracts sufficient followers to permit such an analysis, we may no longer need to look to crowdsourcing platforms to evaluate the system's outputs, and may actually obtain a finer granularity of insight into the kinds of metaphors, oppositions and rendering strategies that humans most appreciate.

7 Lucky Punches

@MetaphorMagnet uses a variety of knowledge sources to formulate its observations and an even wider range of linguistic forms to package them into pithy tweets. Yet in every case it employs the same core strategy: identify a semantic contrast in a knowledge-base; employ semantic reasoning to elaborate a plausible but antagonistic scenario around this central contrast; and use attested Web n-grams to render this scenario in a provocative linguistic form. Though each stage is distinct from an abstract design view, they are all conflated in practice, so that e.g. Web n-grams are also used to *inspire* the system by suggesting the contrasts, juxtapositions and conceptual metaphors that appear most worthy of elaboration.

The use of raw n-grams that a system can only superficially understand constitutes a leap of faith that often pays off but sometimes does not. Consider how the 4-gram "*design is the heart*" (freq=151) provides half of the following tweet:

.@design_scientist says design is a united collaboration
.@design_lover says it is a divided heart
#Design=#Collaboration #Design=#Heart

While a human reader might understand *divided heart* as a poetic allusion to *divided loyalties* – which is nicely antagonistic to the notion of a *united* collaboration – *@MetaphorMagnet* has an altogether more literal understanding of the stereotypical heart, which it knows to be *divided* into various chambers. That the above juxtaposition works well is thus as much a matter of raw luck as deliberate effort, though as the old saying puts it, "*the harder I work the luckier I get*." *@MetaphorMagnet* works hard to earn its frequent good fortune, and so any risk that raw n-grams bring to the generation process is more than compensated for by the unforeseeable resonance that they so often bring with them.

For more detail on the internal workings of *@MetaphorMagnet*, readers are directed to the online resource to RobotComix.com.

Acknowledgements

The author is grateful to the European Commission for funding this work via the WHIM project (The What If Machine; grant number 611560). The author is also grateful for the support of Science Foundation Ireland (SFI) via the *CNGL Centre for Global Intelligent Content*.

References

Barnden, J. A. (2008). Metaphor and artificial intelligence: Why they matter to each other. In R.W. Gibbs, Jr. (Ed.), *The Cambridge Handbook of Metaphor and Thought*, 311-338. Cambridge, UK: Cambridge University Press

Brants, T. and Franz, A. (2006). *Web 1T 5-gram Ver. 1*. Linguistic Data Consortium.

Carbonell, J. G. (1981). Metaphor: An inescapable phenomenon in natural language comprehension. *Report 2404*. Pittsburgh, PA. Carnegie Mellon Computer Science Dept.

Torrance, E. P. (1980). Growing Up Creatively Gifted: The 22-Year Longitudinal Study. *The Creative Child and Adult Quarterly*, 3, 148-158

Gentner, D., Falkenhainer, B. and Skorstad, J. (1989). Metaphor: The Good, The Bad and the Ugly. In *Theoretical Issues in NLP*, Yorick Wilks (Ed.) Hillsdale, NJ: Lawrence Erlbaum Associates.

Glucksberg, S. (1998). Understanding metaphors. *Current Directions in Psychological Science,* 7:39-43.

Guilford, J.P. (1967). *The Nature of Human Intelligence*. New York: McGraw Hill.

Hearst, M. (1992). Automatic acquisition of hyponyms from large text corpora. *In Proc. of the 14th International Conference on Computational Linguistics*, pp 539–545.

Lakoff, G. and Johnson, M. (1980). *Metaphors We Live By*. University of Chicago Press.

Martin, J. H. (1990). A Computational Model of Metaphor Interpretation. New York: Academic Press.

Mason, Z. J. (2004). CorMet: A Computational, Corpus-Based Conventional Metaphor Extraction System, *Computational Linguistics*, 30(1):23-44.

Pollio, H. R. (1996). Boundaries in Humor and Metaphor. J. S. Mio and A. N. Katz (Eds.), *Metaphor: Implications and Applications*. Mahwah, New Jersey: Laurence Erlbaum Associates, 231–253.

Raskin, V. (1985). *Semantic Mechanisms of Humor*. Dordrecht.

Shutova, E. (2010). Metaphor Identification Using Verb and Noun Clustering. In *the Proc. of the 23rd COLING, the International Conference on Computational Linguistics.*

Veale, T. and Hao, Y. (2007). Comprehending and Generating Apt Metaphors: A Web-driven, Case-based Approach to Figurative Language. In *Proc. of the 22nd AAAI conference of the Association for the Advancement of Artificial Intelligence*.

Veale, T. and Li, G. (2011). Creative Introspection and Knowledge Acquisition: Learning about the world thru introspective questions and exploratory metaphors. In Proc. of the 25th AAAI Conf. of the Assoc. for Advancement of A.I., San Francisco.

Veale, T. and Li, G. (2013). Creating Similarity: Lateral Thinking for Vertical Similarity Judgments. *In Proceedings of ACL 2013, the 51st Annual Meeting of the Association for Computational Linguistics,* Sofia, Bulgaria, August 2013.

Author Index

Association for Computational Linguistics
209 N. Eighth Street
Stroudsburg, Pennsylvania 18360

CURRAN ASSOCIATES INC
proceedings
.com